Disclaimer

All erudition contained in this book is given for informational and educational purposes only. The author is not in any way accountable for any results or outcomes that emanate from using this material. Constructive attempts have been made to provide information that is both accurate and effective, but the author is not bound for the accuracy or use/misuse of this information.

Gnostic Gospels Collection

The Forbidden Knowledge - The Lost Apocryphal Gospels of Mary Magdalene, Jude, Philip, Thomas and John

Henrich W. Harris

Contents

The Gnostic Gospel of Thomas 7

    Introduction 7

Gospel of Thomas on Christianity and Spirituality............................... 9

Difference between Gospel of Thomas and other Gnostic Gospels ... 11

    Proponents and Opposition of the Gospel of Thomas 14

The Gospel and the Secret saying of Jesus 18

    Part one 20

    Part two 24

    Part three 26

    Part Four 28

Jesus' sayings to Thomas 32

Parables and Saying 38

    Trinity 42

    Spirit 44

    Hell 48

Contextual interpretation of Jesus's sayings 50

    Biblical text Abbreviations 65

The Gospel of Mary Magdalene - The First Apostle Woman 67

    Introduction 67

Dialogue, Message and teachings in the Gospel 73

The Possessed 75

EXORCISM 89

Jesus Teachings in the Gospel of Mary 106

    The Body and the Word 110

Controversy over the Gospel of Mary 116

The Gospel and acceptance into early Christianity 122

Comparison of the Gospel of Mary with other Gospel books 124

The History of Christianity 144

Mary Magdalene's Works 150

Mary Magdalene and Jesus's Movement................................ 158

MARY AT JESUS RESURRECTION AND TRANSFIGURATION.... 161

The Apocryphal and Gnostic Gospel of Judas............................ 173

Gnostic and Apocryphal Gospel of Philip: A Deep Dive............ 207

The Significance of the Gospel of Philip in Gnostic Literature 207

The Gospel of Philip: An Overview... 209

Sacraments and Rituals in the Gospel of Philip............................ 211

The Nature of Reality: Gnostic Cosmology in the Gospel of Philip 213

The Mystery of Resurrection in the Gospel of Philip.................... 215

Jesus in the Gospel of Philip... 217

The Bridal Chamber: Symbolism and Significance in the Gospel of Philip.. 219

The Role of Light and Darkness in the Gospel of Philip 221

The Gnostic Church vs. Orthodox Christianity in the Gospel of Philip
.... 223

The Language and Imagery of the Gospel of Philip.................... 225

The Historical Context of the Gospel of Philip 227

The Legacy of the Gospel of Philip 229

Controversies and Debates in the Gospel of Philip 231

The Gospel of Philip in Art and Culture 233

Modern Gnosticism and the Gospel of Philip............................... 235

Conclusion: The Timeless Wisdom of the Gospel of Philip........... 237

The Gnostic Gospel of Thomas

Introduction

The Gospel of Thomas is a Gnostic gospel that was discovered in 1945 in Nag Hammadi, Egypt. It consists of 114 sayings or logia attributed to the Master, "the Living Jesus," without any narrative or biographical information, and written down by Didymus Judas Thomas, the Twin. Who was Thomas, the Twin? Was he Jesus' alter ego or closest disciple? The Gospel of Thomas is an important text for understanding Gnosticism, a religious movement that was popular in the early Christian period. The Gospel of Thomas is written in Coptic, an Egyptian language that was spoken during the time of the Roman Empire. The original composition of the gospel is believed to have been in Greek, although no complete version in that language has ever been discovered. The text is believed to have been written sometime in the 2nd century CE.

Among the fifty-three manuscripts, Codex II contains a gospel attributed to Jesus' disciple Thomas. This gospel does not contain apocalyptic proclamations or prophecies. Instead, it reveals an infinite space that exists both within and outside of us. All we need to do is break open the man-made jar that hides it from us.

Some view the Gospel of Thomas as the "protogospel" that we have been seeking, the only one that transmits the authentic words of Jesus. However, Jesus of Nazareth was not a writer, so it is impossible to speak of "the authentic words of Jesus." Every saying we possess consists of words that have been heard, which bear the imprint of a listener whose listening may be crude or subtle.

The gospels of Mark, Matthew, Luke, John, Thomas, and others represent at least five different ways of listening to the Word. Each also represents different ways of understanding, interpreting, and translating cultural and linguistic differences according to the quality of his own intimacy with the Master, and according to his own levels of evolution, openness, and awareness.

The sayings in the Gospel of Thomas often present Jesus as a teacher of wisdom, rather than a miracle worker or savior. Many of the sayings are similar to those found in the canonical gospels of Matthew, Mark, Luke, and John, but are presented in a more cryptic and enigmatic manner. Some of the sayings in the Gospel of Thomas appear to contradict or challenge the teachings of the canonical gospels.

The Gospel of Thomas was not included in the canon of the New Testament, and its status as a sacred text is disputed among Christian denominations. However, it has gained popularity among scholars and spiritual seekers interested in Gnosticism, mysticism, and alternative interpretations of Christianity.

Gospel of Thomas on Christianity and Spirituality

The Gospel of Thomas is a text that is not included in the canon of Christian scripture. It has been the subject of much debate and attention among Christian scholars. The text is classified as a "sayings gospel," which means that it primarily consists of collections of teachings or sayings attributed to Jesus, rather than a narrative of his life and ministry.

The Gospel of Thomas is believed by many scholars to reflect the teachings of the Gnostic movement. The Gnostics emphasized secret knowledge or gnosis as a path to salvation, and this influence is seen in the text's emphasis on the attainment of knowledge and spiritual insight.

Some of the sayings in the Gospel of Thomas share similarities with teachings found in other religious traditions, such as Buddhism and Hinduism. This has led some scholars to speculate that there may have been cross-cultural influence or borrowing between these traditions.

The Gospel of Thomas includes several sayings that are not found in any of the canonical gospels. These unique sayings have been interpreted as promoting a radical egalitarianism or even a rejection of traditional family structures.

Scholars have debated the authenticity of the Gospel of Thomas. While some argue that the sayings in the text can be traced back to an earlier source, others contend that the text was written later and contains interpolations or additions.

Despite its non-canonical status, the Gospel of Thomas has had an impact on Christian theology and spirituality, particularly in the areas of mysticism and esotericism. Some have even argued that it represents a more authentic or original form of Christianity than the canonical gospels.

The Gospel of Thomas remains a fascinating and contentious subject for scholars and anyone interested in the history and evolution of Christianity. The Gospel of Thomas emphasizes the importance of inner spiritual growth and knowledge or gnosis as a path to salvation. This has influenced Christian mysticism, which places greater emphasis on personal experience and direct communion with God than traditional Christian theology.

The Gospel of Thomas also challenges traditional Christian teachings and structures, promoting radical egalitarianism and rejecting the traditional family structure. This has led to debates about the role of hierarchy and power within the Christian church and the nature of relationships and family structures. The inclusion of unique sayings in the Gospel of Thomas has led scholars to reconsider the history and evolution of Christianity, particularly the development of the canon of the New Testament. Some scholars argue that the Gospel of Thomas represents a more authentic or original form of Christianity that was suppressed or excluded from the canonical gospels. Overall, the Gospel of Thomas has had a significant impact on Christian theology and spirituality, challenging traditional beliefs and structures and emphasizing the importance of personal spiritual experience and direct communion with the divine.

Unlike the canonical gospels, which portray women in more limited roles, the Gospel of Thomas features several sayings in which women are prominent figures and are portrayed as having equal access to divine knowledge and salvation. This has led to a reassessment of the role of women in early Christianity and has prompted discussions about the ways in which women have been marginalized in the history of the Christian church. Moreover, the Gospel of Thomas has prompted a renewed interest in the examination of early Christian literature, along with further investigation of the early Christian interpretation and implementation of their beliefs. Its incorporation of sayings that are comparable to those found in other religious traditions has also helped to deepen our comprehension of the cross-cultural impacts and interactions that transpired during the early stages of Christianity.

Difference between Gospel of Thomas and other Gnostic Gospels

The Gospel of Thomas differs significantly from other Gnostic gospels, while still sharing similarities in themes and teachings. One key difference is its form, consisting primarily of sayings attributed to Jesus, in contrast to other Gnostic gospels such as the Gospel of Mary and the Gospel of Philip, which contain more narrative elements and stories.

In addition to its form, the Gospel of Thomas also stands out in terms of its tone. While other Gnostic gospels often emphasize the dualistic nature of the universe and the struggle between the material and spiritual worlds, the Gospel of Thomas is more focused on the individual's inner spiritual journey and the attainment of knowledge or gnosis as a path to salvation. Despite these differences, the Gospel of Thomas shares similarities with other Gnostic texts in its emphasis on the importance of inner spiritual knowledge and the idea that the material world is illusory. However, it differs from other Gnostic texts in its positive view of the physical world and its emphasis on the role of the individual in achieving spiritual enlightenment.

Moreover, the Gospel of Thomas portrays Jesus as a sage or philosopher imparting wisdom and guidance to his followers, in contrast to other Gnostic gospels such as the Gospel of Judas and the Gospel of Mary, which depict Jesus as a secret teacher who imparts hidden knowledge to his disciples. Overall, the Gospel of Thomas is a unique and valuable document in its form, tone, and emphasis on the individual's spiritual journey, while still being part of the greater Gnostic tradition with shared themes and teachings.

In the Gospel of Thomas and other Gnostic gospels, the apostles play a different role. Rather than being presented as central figures or intermediaries between Jesus and his followers, the Gospel of Thomas portrays Jesus as a teacher who imparts wisdom and knowledge to all of his disciples, without giving special treatment to the apostles. This portrayal contrasts with other Gnostic gospels, such as the Gospel of Judas, which present the apostles as flawed or inferior, compared to other disciples who receive secret teachings from Jesus.

Moreover, the Gospel of Thomas emphasizes the importance of self-discovery and individual experience. Instead of relying on external authorities or institutions for guidance and knowledge, the text encourages readers to seek knowledge and truth within themselves. This emphasis on the individual's personal experience and relationship with the divine distinguishes the Gospel of Thomas from some other Gnostic gospels, which may place more emphasis on esoteric knowledge and secret teachings.

Although the Gospel of Thomas shares some similarities with other Gnostic texts in presenting Jesus as a divine figure, it is notable for its lack of emphasis on Jesus' death and resurrection as central to salvation. This contrasts with mainstream Christianity, which emphasizes the death and resurrection of Jesus as the means of redemption. The Gospel of Thomas instead focuses on the individual's attainment of spiritual enlightenment through inner knowledge and understanding.

The Gospel of Thomas shares several key themes and concepts with other Gnostic gospels. These include emphasizing the importance of secret or esoteric knowledge, portraying Jesus as a divine or spiritual figure who reveals this knowledge to his followers, adopting a dualistic worldview that views the world as a battleground between opposing forces of light and darkness, and rejecting traditional religious authority and hierarchy in favor of individual spiritual experience and insight.

One of the most significant similarities between the Gospel of Thomas and other Gnostic texts is their emphasis on the importance of secret or esoteric knowledge as a means of achieving spiritual enlightenment and salvation. Gnostic texts imply that a hidden or secret wisdom can be achieved by those initiated into the right teachings and practices. The Gospel of Thomas contains several sayings that imply the importance of seeking out hidden knowledge and understanding to achieve spiritual growth and enlightenment.

Another similarity between the Gospel of Thomas and other Gnostic texts is the portrayal of Jesus as a divine or spiritual figure who reveals this secret knowledge to his followers. In the Gospel of Thomas, Jesus is presented as a teacher or guide who imparts a special wisdom that is not available to others. This concept of Jesus as a divine or spiritual figure who is distinct from the human Jesus of history is a common theme in many Gnostic texts.

The Gospel of Thomas also shares with other Gnostic texts a dualistic worldview, which views the world as a battleground between opposing forces of light and darkness, spirit and matter, or good and evil. The Gospel of Thomas suggests that the material world is a realm of darkness and ignorance, from which the soul must be liberated to achieve salvation.

Many Gnostic texts, including the Gospel of Thomas, reject traditional religious authority and hierarchy, emphasizing instead the importance of individual spiritual experience and insight. They suggest that the path to spiritual enlightenment is not through external institutions or doctrines, but through personal exploration and discovery. In this way, the Gospel of Thomas shares with other Gnostic texts a tendency to question and challenge established religious traditions and beliefs with confidence.

Proponents and Opposition of the Gospel of Thomas

The Gospel of Thomas is a valuable resource for understanding the diversity of early Christian thought and spirituality. Proponents argue that it provides a different perspective on Jesus and his teachings than the canonical gospels, which were largely shaped by the theological and political concerns of the early Christian church. Some proponents of the Gospel of Thomas even argue that it represents a more authentic or original form of Christianity than the canonical gospels. They point to the fact that the Gospel of Thomas is a collection of sayings attributed to Jesus, rather than a narrative of his life and ministry. This emphasis on the teachings of Jesus reflects an early period of Christianity, before the church became centralized and began to codify its beliefs.

Some people find the Gospel of Thomas useful for exploring the history of Christian mysticism and esotericism. This is because it contains many sayings that stress the importance of inner spiritual experience and personal transformation, reflecting a tradition of Christian spirituality that emphasizes direct personal experience of the divine over institutionalized religious authority. Others are inspired by the Gospel of Thomas for their own spiritual practice. They see in its teachings a call for deeper self-awareness and a more compassionate and inclusive approach to life. The focus on inner spiritual experience and personal transformation is taken as a strong message for contemporary spiritual seekers.

The Gospel of Thomas is highly regarded by its proponents for its distinctive perspective on Jesus and his teachings, its emphasis on inner spiritual experience, and its ability to inspire new forms of Christian spirituality and theology. Despite ongoing debates regarding its authenticity and origin, the gospel has undoubtedly had a significant impact on Christian thought and practice. Opposition to the Gospel of Thomas has persisted since its discovery, coming from a variety of sources.

One of the primary criticisms aimed at the Gospel of Thomas is its absence of narrative context. Unlike the canonical gospels, which give a thorough account of Jesus' life, teachings, and ministry, the Gospel of Thomas is solely comprised of a collection of sayings attributed to Jesus. Some critics contend that this makes it hard to interpret the sayings in their original setting, and that it results in a fragmented and incomplete comprehension of Jesus' message.

Others have raised concerns about the Gnostic elements found in the Gospel of Thomas. Gnosticism was a spiritual movement that emerged in the early centuries of Christianity, characterized by a belief in secret knowledge or gnosis as a path to salvation. Gnostic ideas were generally rejected by mainstream Christianity as heretical, and some scholars argue that the Gospel of Thomas reflects this Gnostic influence. Critics contend that this makes the text incompatible with orthodox Christian theology, and that it undermines the authority of the canonical gospels.

Another criticism of the Gospel of Thomas is its emphasis on individual spiritual experience at the expense of community and social engagement. Some scholars argue that the text encourages a kind of individualistic spirituality that could lead to a neglect of social justice and a lack of concern for the common good. Critics contend that this is contrary to the teachings of Jesus as found in the canonical gospels, which emphasize the importance of loving one's neighbor and caring for the marginalized and oppressed. Finally, it should be noted that some religious leaders and theologians have expressed concern over the Gospel of Thomas' popularity among certain segments of the Christian community.

They fear that it could lead to a fragmentation of the faith and a rejection of traditional Christian teachings and practices. However, it is important to acknowledge that the Gospel of Thomas promotes a form of spiritual individualism that is in line with early Christian thought and spirituality.

While Christian worship is communal in nature and the church is a community of believers, the Gospel of Thomas still holds value for many scholars and spiritual seekers seeking to explore the diversity of early Christian thought and spirituality.

Although it is unlikely to be accepted as authoritative by mainstream Christian denominations due to its non-canonical status, its teachings continue to inspire new forms of Christian spirituality and theology.

The Gospel and the Secret saying of Jesus

Prologue

These are the secret sayings that the living Jesus spoke and Judas Thomas recorded.

He said, "Whoever finds the interpretation of these sayings will not taste death."

Jesus said, "Let one who seeks not stop seeking until one finds. When one finds, one will be disturbed. When one is disturbed, one will be amazed, and will reign over all."

Jesus said, "If your leaders say to you, 'Behold, the kingdom is in the sky,' then the birds in the sky will get there before you. If they say to you, 'It is in the sea,' then the fish will get there before you. Rather, the kingdom is inside you and outside you. When you know yourselves, then you will be known, and will understand that you are children of the living Father. But if you do not know yourselves, then you live in poverty, and embody poverty."

Jesus said, "The older person many days old will not hesitate to ask a little child seven days old about the realm of life, and this person will live. For many of the first will be last, and will become a single one."

Jesus said, "Know what is within your sight, and what is hidden from you will become clear to you. For there is nothing hidden that will not be revealed."

His disciples asked him and said, "Do you want us to fast? How shall we pray? Shall we give to charity? What food may we eat?" Jesus said, "Do not lie or do what you dislike, since all things are clear before heaven. For there is nothing hidden that will not be revealed, and nothing covered that will not be uncovered."

Jesus said, "Blessed is the lion that the human eats, so that the lion becomes human. Cursed is the human that the lion eats, so that the lion becomes human."

He said, "A person is like a wise fisher who cast a net into the sea, and drew it up from the sea full of little fish. Among them the wise fisher discovered a fine big fish. So the fisher threw all the little fish back into the sea, and with no hesitation kept the big fish. Whoever has ears to hear ought to listen."

Jesus said, "Behold, the sower went out, took a handful of seeds, and scattered them. Some fell on the road, and the birds came and ate them. Others fell on rock, and they did not take root in the soil or produce any heads of grain. Others fell among thorns, and the thorns choked the seeds and worms consumed them. Still others fell on good soil, and brought forth a good crop: it yielded sixty per measure and one hundred twenty per measure."

Jesus said, "I have come to bring fire to the world, and how I wish it were already kindled! But I have a baptism to undergo, and what constraint I am under until it is completed! Do you think I came to bring peace on earth? No, I tell you, but division. From now on there will be five in one family divided against each other, three against two and two against three. They will be divided, father against son and son against father, mother against daughter and daughter against mother, mother-in-law against daughter-in-law and daughter-in-law against mother-in-law."

Part one

Jesus said, "This heaven will pass away, and the one above it will pass away. The dead are not alive, and the living will not die. In the days when you consumed what is dead, you made it alive. When you come to dwell in the light, what will you do? On the day when you were one, you became two. But when you become two, what will you do?"

The disciples said to Jesus, "We know that you will depart from us. Who will be our leader?" Jesus said to them, "No matter where you are, you are to go to James the Just, for whose sake heaven and earth came into being."

Jesus said to his disciples, "Compare me to someone and tell me whom I am like." Simon Peter said to him, "You are like a just messenger." Matthew said to him, "You are like a wise philosopher." Thomas said to him, "Teacher, my mouth is utterly unable to say whom you are like." Jesus said, "I am not your teacher. Because you have drunk, you have become intoxicated from the bubbling spring that I have tended." And he took Thomas and withdrew, and spoke to him three sayings. When Thomas came back to his friends, they asked him, "What did Jesus say to you?" Thomas said to them, "If I tell you one of the sayings he spoke to me, you will pick up rocks and stone me. Then fire will come forth from the rocks and devour you."

Jesus said, "If you fast, you will bring sin upon yourselves. If you pray, you will be condemned. If you give to charity, you will harm your spirits. When you go into any land and wander from region to region, and people welcome you, eat what they serve you and heal the sick among them. For what goes into your mouth will not defile you, but that which issues from your mouth - it is that which will defile you."

Jesus said, "When you see one who was not born of woman, fall on your faces and worship. That one is your father."

The disciples said to Jesus, "Tell us, what is the kingdom of heaven like?" He said to them, "It is like a mustard seed, the smallest of all seeds, but when it falls on prepared soil, it produces a great plant and becomes a shelter for the birds of heaven."

Jesus said, "I will give you what no eye has seen, what no ear has heard, what no hand has touched, what has not arisen in the human heart."

The disciples said to Jesus, "Tell us, how will our end come?" Jesus said, "Have you discovered the beginning, then, that you are looking for the end? For where the beginning is, there will the end be. Blessed is the one who stands at the beginning, for that one will know the end and will not taste death."

Jesus said, "Blessed is one who existed before coming into being. If you become my disciples and listen to my words, these stones will serve you. For there are five trees in Paradise which remain undisturbed summer and winter and whose leaves do not fall. Whoever becomes acquainted with them will not experience death."

Mary asked Jesus, "Who are your disciples like?"
Jesus replied, "They are like little children living in a field that is not their own. When the owners of the field come, they will say, 'Give our field back to us.' The children will take off their clothes in the presence of the owners and return the field to them.
"For this reason, I say: If the owner of a house knows that a thief is coming, the owner will be on guard before the thief arrives and will not let the thief break into the house and steal their possessions.
"As for you, be on guard against the world. Gird yourselves and prepare for action so that robbers will not find a way to prevail against you. The trouble you expect will come.
"Let there be among you a person who understands. When the crop ripens, a reaper comes quickly with a sickle in hand and harvests it. Whoever has ears to hear ought to listen."

Jesus saw some nursing babies and said to his disciples, "These nursing babies are like those who enter the kingdom."

They said to him, "Then shall we enter the kingdom as babies?"

Jesus said to them,

"When you make the two into one, when you make the inner like the outer and the outer like the inner, and the upper like the lower, when you make male and female into a single one, so that the male will not be male and the female will not be female, when you make eyes replacing an eye, a hand replacing a hand, a foot replacing a foot, and an image replacing an image, then you will enter the kingdom."

Jesus said, "I shall choose one from a thousand and two from ten thousand, and they will stand as a single one."

His disciples said, "Show us the place where you are, for we must seek it."

He said to them, "Whoever has ears ought to listen. There is light within an enlightened person, and it shines on the whole world. If the light does not shine, it is dark."

Jesus said, "Love your companion like your life, protect such a one like the pupil of your eye.

Jesus said, "You see the speck that is in your companion's eye, but you do not see the beam that is in your own eye. When you take the beam out of your own eye, then you will see well enough to take the speck out of your companion's eye.

"If you do not fast from the world, you will not find the kingdom. If you do not keep the Sabbath a Sabbath, you will not see the Father."

Jesus said, "I took my stand in the middle of the world, and in the flesh I appeared to people. I found them all drunk, and I did not find any of them thirsty. My soul ached for these human children because they are blind of heart and do not see that they came into the world empty, and they also seek to depart from the world empty. But now they are drunk. When they become sober, then they will repent."

Jesus said, "If the flesh came into being because of spirit, it is amazing, but if spirit came into being because of the body, it is even more amazing. I am amazed though, at how such great wealth has settled into such poverty."

Jesus said, "Where there are three deities, they are divine. Where there are two or one, I am present."

Jesus said, "A prophet is not popular in their hometown, and a doctor does not heal family and friends."

Part two

Jesus' Teachings

Jesus said, "A grapevine that is not healthy will be pulled up by its roots and destroyed."

Jesus said, "Those who have something in hand will be given more, and those who have nothing will be deprived even of the tiny bit they have."

Jesus said, "Be wanderers."

His disciples asked him, "Who are you to say these things to us?"

"You do not know who I am from what I say to you. Instead, you have become like the Jews: either loving the tree but hating its fruit, or loving the fruit but hating the tree."

Jesus said, "Whoever blasphemes against the Father or the Child will be forgiven. But whoever blasphemes against the holy Spirit will not be forgiven, either on earth or in heaven."

Jesus said, "Good fruit cannot come from thorn bushes or thistles, for such plants yield no fruit. A good person brings forth good from the storehouse, while a bad person brings forth evil from the corrupt storehouse in the heart, and says evil things. For from the abundance of the heart, this person brings forth evil."

Jesus said, "From Adam to John the Baptist, among those born of women, no one is greater than John the Baptist. Yet I have said that whoever among you becomes like a child will know the kingdom and will become greater than John."

Jesus said, "A person cannot mount two horses or bend two bows, and a servant cannot serve two lords. That servant would respect one and offend the other. A person does not drink aged wine and immediately want to drink new wine. New wine is not poured into aged wineskins, for the skins may break, and aged wine is not poured into new wineskins, for the wine may spoil. An old patch is not sewn onto a new piece of clothing, for there would be a rip."

Jesus said, "If two make peace with each other in a single house, they will say to the mountain, 'Move!' and it will move."

Jesus said, "Blessed are those who are alone and chosen, for they will find the kingdom. For they have come from it, and they will return there again."

Jesus said, "If someone asks you, 'Where have you come from?' say to them, 'We have come from the light, where the light came into being by itself, established itself, and appeared in an image of light.' If they ask you, 'Are you the light?' say, 'We are its and we are the chosen of the living Father.' If they ask you, 'What is the evidence of your Father in you?' tell them, 'It is motion and rest.'"

His disciples asked him, "When will the final rest for the dead take place and when will the new world come?" He said to them, "What you look for has already come, but you do not know it."

His disciples said to him, "Twenty-four prophets have spoken in Israel, and they all spoke of you." He said to them, "You have ignored the Living One who is with you and have spoken only of the dead."

His disciples asked him, "Is circumcision useful or not?" He said to them, "If it were useful, a father would produce children who are already circumcised from their mother. Rather, the true, spiritual circumcision is useful in every respect."

Jesus said, "Blessed are the poor, for theirs is the kingdom of heaven."

Part three

Sayings of Jesus

Jesus said, "Two people will relax on a couch: one will die, one will live."
Salome asked, "Who are you, sir? You sat on my couch and ate from my table as if you are somebody."
Jesus answered, "I am from the One who is whole, I was granted my Father's estate."
Salome replied, "I am your disciple."
Jesus said, "For this reason I say: one who is whole will be filled with light, but one who is fragmented will be filled with darkness."

Jesus said, "I disclose my mysteries to those who are worthy. Do not let your left hand know what your right hand is doing."

Jesus told a story, "There was a rich farmer who had a great deal of money. The farmer said, 'I shall invest my money so that I may sow, reap, plant, and fill my storehouses with produce. Then I shall have everything.' These were the plans, but that very night the farmer died. Whoever has ears ought to listen."

Jesus said, "A certain person was entertaining guests. When dinner was ready, the host sent a servant to invite the guests. "The servant went to the first one and said, 'My lord invites you.' "The guest said, 'Some merchants owe me money, and they are coming to me tonight. I must go to give instructions to them. Please excuse me from dinner.' "The servant went to another guest and said, 'My lord invites you.' "The guest said, 'I have bought a house, and I have been called away for the day. I have no time.' "The servant went to another guest and said, 'My lord invites you.' "The guest said, 'My friend is to be married, and I must arrange the dinner, so I shall not be able to come. Please excuse me from dinner.' "The servant went to yet another guest and said, 'My lord invites you.'

"The guest said, 'I have bought a farm, and I am going to collect the rent, so I shall not be able to come. Please excuse me.' "The servant returned and said to the lord, "Those whom you invited to dinner have asked to be excused.' "The lord said to the servant, 'Go out on the streets, and bring back whomever you find to eat my dinner.' "Businesspeople and merchants will not enter the realm of my Father."

He said, "There was a good person who owned a vineyard. The owner rented it to some farmers, that the farmers might work in it and the owner might collect the profits from them. The owner sent a servant, that the farmers might turn over the profits from the vineyard, but instead they seized, beat, and almost killed the servant. So the servant returned and told the lord. The lord said, 'Perhaps the servant did not know them.' "The owner sent another servant, and the farmers beat that one, too. "Then the lord sent his child and said, 'Perhaps they will show my child some respect.' But since the farmers knew that the child was the heir to the vineyard, they seized and killed the child. "Whoever has ears ought to listen."

Jesus said, "Show me the stone the builders rejected: that is the cornerstone."

Jesus said, "Whoever knows everything but lacks within lacks everything."

Jesus said, "Blessed are you when you are hated and persecuted, and no one will discover the place where you have been persecuted."

Part Four

Jesus said, "Whoever is close to me is close to the fire, and whoever is far from me is far from the kingdom."

Jesus said, "Images are visible to people, but the light within is hidden in the Father's image of light. He will reveal himself, but his image is hidden by his light."

Jesus said, "When you see a likeness of yourself, you are happy. But when you see your images that came into being before you, and that neither die nor become visible, how much you will be able to tolerate!"

Jesus said, "Adam came from great power and great wealth, but he was not worthy of you. For if he had been worthy, he would not have tasted death."

Jesus said, "Foxes have dens and birds have nests, but the Child of Humanity has no place to lay his head and rest." Jesus said, "Miserable is the body that depends on another body, and miserable is the soul that depends on the two of them." Jesus said, "The angels and the prophets will come to you and give you what is yours. You, in turn, give them what you have, and say to yourselves, 'When will they come and take what is theirs?'"

Jesus said, "Why do you wash the outside of the cup? Do you not understand that the one who made the inside also made the outside?" Jesus said, "Come to me, for my yoke is easy and my lordship is gentle, and you will find rest for yourselves." They said to him, "Tell us who you are so we can believe in you." He said to them, "You study the face of the sky and the earth, but you have not come to know the one who is before you, and you do not know how to study this moment."

Jesus said, "Seek and you will find. In the past I did not answer all your questions. Now I am willing to answer them, but you no longer ask.

Jesus said, "Do not give what is holy to dogs, for they may drop it on a manure pile. Do not throw pearls to swine, for they may make them worthless." Jesus said, "Whoever seeks will find, whoever knocks will be let in."

Jesus said, "If you have money, do not lend it at interest. Rather, give it to someone who will not return it." Jesus said, "The kingdom of the Father is like a woman who took a little yeast, hid it in dough, and made large loaves of bread. Whoever has ears ought to listen."

Jesus said, "The kingdom of the Father is like a woman who was carrying a jar full of flour. While she was walking on a road far from home, the handle of the jar broke and the flour spilled behind her on the road. She did not know it: she had not noticed the problem. When she reached her house, she put the jar down and discovered that it was empty." Jesus said, "The kingdom of the Father is like someone who wanted to put a powerful person to death. He drew his sword at home and thrust it into a wall to find out whether his hand would go through. Then he killed the powerful one."

The disciples said to him, "Your brothers and your mother are standing outside." He said to them, "Those here who do the will of my Father are my brothers and my mother. They will enter the kingdom of my Father." Jesus said, "The kingdom of heaven is like a shepherd who had a large sheep that wandered away. The shepherd left the ninety-nine and searched for that one until it was found. After going to such trouble, the shepherd said to the sheep, 'I love you more than the ninety-nine.' " Jesus said, "Whoever listens to my teaching and follows it will be like me, and I shall be that person, and what is hidden will be revealed to that one."

Jesus said, "The kingdom of heaven is like a person who owned a field but did not know that a treasure was hidden in it. At death, the owner left the field to his child. The child did not know about the treasure either but took over the field and sold it.

The buyer went plowing and found the treasure and began to lend money at interest to whomever he pleased." Jesus said, "Let the person who finds the world and becomes rich renounce the world." Jesus said, "The heavens and the earth will pass away before you, but whoever is living in union with the Living One will not see death nor fear." Jesus said, "The person who discovers their true self is worth more than the world."

Jesus said, "Woe to the one who relies on the body and forgets the soul! Woe to the one who relies on the soul and forgets the body!" His disciples asked him, "When will the kingdom come?" Jesus replied, "It will not come by searching for it. Nor will it do to say, 'Here it is!' or 'There it is!' Rather, the kingdom of the Father is spread out on the earth, but people do not see it." Simon Peter said to them, "Let Mary leave us, because women are not worthy of life." Jesus said, "I will guide her so that she too may become a living spirit like you men. For every woman who makes herself like a man will enter the kingdom of heaven."

Jesus' sayings to Thomas

As we walked and listened to the secret sayings that the Savior spoke to Judas Thomas, he said confidently, "Brother Thomas, while you still have time in the world, listen to me and I shall explain what you have been reflecting upon in your mind. "Since it is said that you are my twin and my true friend, examine yourself and understand who you are, how you live, and what will become of you. As you are called my brother, ignorance about yourself is not acceptable. You understand some things, for already you understand that I am the knowledge of truth. While walking with me, though you are ignorant of other things, already you have obtained knowledge, and you will be described as one who knows self. Whoever does not know self does not know anything, but whoever knows self already has acquired knowledge about the depth of the universe. So, my brother Thomas, you have seen what is hidden from people, what they stumble over in their ignorance."

Thomas asked the Savior to tell him about the things that are hidden and cannot be seen. The Savior explained, "All the bodies of humans and animals are irrational from birth. Indeed, this is clear from the way a creature … Beings that come from above, however, do not live like the creatures you can see. Rather, they derive their life from their own root, and their crop provides nourishment for them. On the other hand, these bodies you can see feed on creatures like them, and for this reason they are subject to change. Whatever is subject to change will perish and be lost, and has no more hope of life, because this body is an animal body. Just as animal bodies perish, so also will these figures perish. Are they not the result of copulation, like animal bodies? If this kind of body, too, is the result of copulation, how can it give birth to anything different from the animals? For this reason, then, you are babies until you attain perfection."

Thomas then related to the Lord that people who speak about what is invisible and hard to explain are like archers who shoot arrows at a target during the night.

Of course, they shoot arrows like any other archers, since they are shooting at a target, but in this case the target cannot be seen. When the light comes forth, however, and banishes the darkness, then what each person has done will become clear. "You are our light, and you bring enlightenment, Lord." Jesus said, "Light dwells in light." Thomas asked, "Lord, why does this visible light that shines upon people rise and set?" The Savior said, "Blessed Thomas, this visible light shines upon you not to keep you here, but to make you leave."

Thomas said, "Lord, I am asking for your help because I believe that you can assist us, as you have said." The Savior replied, "I am speaking to you because you are capable of understanding this instruction meant for the wise. To attain perfection, you must adhere to these teachings. If you do not, you will remain ignorant. A wise person cannot associate with a fool. The wise person is perfect in all wisdom, while to the fool, good and evil are the same. The wise person is nourished by truth and is like a tree growing by a river.

"Some individuals possess wings yet chase after illusions that are far from truth. The fire that guides them gives an illusion of truth and shines on them with temporary beauty. It makes them prisoners of the pleasures of darkness and captures them in sweet-smelling desires. It blinds them with unquenchable passion, inflames their souls, and becomes like a stake that is jammed into their hearts and cannot be removed. It is like a bit in the mouth, directing them as it wishes.

"This fire has bound these people with its chains, and tied all their limbs with the bitter bond of desire for visible things, which change, decay, and fluctuate impulsively. They are always dragged downwards. When they die, they join all the filthy animals."

Thomas replied, "This is clear and has been said." The Savior replied, "Blessed is the wise person who seeks truth. When one finds it, one rests upon it forever and is not afraid of those who seek to disturb them."

Thomas asked, "Lord, is it beneficial for us to find rest among our own people?" The Savior answered, "Yes, it is beneficial for you because what is visible in human existence will pass away. The fleshly body of people will disintegrate, and when it does, it will find its place in what is visible and can be seen.

"Then the fire that those people see will make them suffer because of their love for the faith they once had. They will be brought back to the visible realm. Moreover, those people who can see in the invisible realm will be consumed without that first love due to their concern about life and the raging of the fire.

"There is little time before what you can see passes away. Then shapeless ghosts will come and live in the tombs among the corpses, forever bringing pain and destruction of the soul." Thomas asked, "What can we say in the face of these things? What should we say to people who are blind? What instruction should we give these miserable mortals? They say, 'We have come to do good, not to curse,' but add, 'If we had not been born in the flesh, we would not have known about sin.'"

The Savior said, "This is true. Do not think of them as human beings, but consider them as animals. For as animals devour each other, so also do people like this devour each other. "Moreover, the kingdom is taken from them because they love the pleasures of fire. They are slaves of death and revel in filth. They satisfy the desires of their parents. These people will be thrown down into hell, beaten as their bitter, wicked natures deserve. They will be whipped to drive them down to the unknown, leaving the limbs of their bodies behind, not with courage but with despair. "Yet these people, being foolish and mad, are happy in the anxieties of this life. Some of those who rush into this madness do not realize they are foolish, but think they are wise. They are drawn to the beauty of the body, as if it would not perish. Their minds turn to themselves, their thoughts are on their own pursuits, but the fire will consume them."

Thomas asked, "Lord, what will happen to those who are cast down in this manner? I fear for them, as many forces oppose them." The Savior answered, "Do you not also have a visible life?" Judas, called Thomas, said, "Lord, you should speak, and I should listen." The Savior answered, "Listen to what I shall say to you, and believe in the truth. What sows and what is sown will pass away in fire, in fire and water, and will be hidden in dark tombs. After a long time the fruit of wicked trees will appear, and will be punished and slaughtered in animal and human mouths, at the instigation of the rain, the wind, the air, and the light shining above."

Thomas answered, "You have convinced us, Lord. We have come to this realization, and now it is clear: this is as it is, and your word is sufficient for us. But these sayings that you utter are laughable and ridiculous to the world, for they are misunderstood. How can we go forth and preach them, since the world does not respect us?" The Savior said, "I tell you the truth: whoever speaks against the Father or Son will be forgiven, but whoever speaks against the Holy Spirit will not be forgiven, either on earth or in heaven. So, speak openly about what you hear in secret. Don't be afraid of those who can only kill the body. Instead, fear the one who can destroy both soul and body in hell. Aren't two sparrows sold for a penny? Yet not one of them falls to the ground without your Father's care. And even the hairs on your head are all counted. So don't be afraid; you are worth more than many sparrows.

"Whoever acknowledges me before others, I will acknowledge before my Father in heaven. But whoever denies me before others, I will deny before my Father in heaven. Don't think that I came to bring peace to the earth. I didn't come to bring peace, but a sword. I came to turn a man against his father, a daughter against her mother, and a daughter-in-law against her mother-in-law. A man's enemies will be the members of his own household.

"Anyone who loves their father or mother more than me is not worthy of me; anyone who loves their son or daughter more than me is not worthy of me. Whoever does not take up their cross and follow me is not worthy of me.

Whoever finds their life will lose it, and whoever loses their life for my sake will find it. "Anyone who welcomes you welcomes me, and anyone who welcomes me welcomes the one who sent me. Whoever welcomes a prophet as a prophet will receive a prophet's reward, and whoever welcomes a righteous person as a righteous person will receive a righteous person's reward. And if anyone gives even a cup of cold water to one of these little ones who is my disciple, truly I tell you, that person will certainly not lose their reward."

"The sun and the moon will give a sweet smell to you, and to the air, the spirit, the earth, and the water. "For if the sun does not shine on these bodies, they will waste away and die like weeds or grass. If the sun shines on weeds, they become vigorous and can choke a grapevine. But if a grapevine becomes vigorous, casts its shadow over the weeds and all the rest of the brush growing along with it, and spreads and flourishes, the grapevine alone inherits the land where it grows and dominates wherever it casts its
shadow. When it grows, then, it dominates the whole land, produces abundantly, and makes the lord even happier. For the lord would have suffered much because of
these weeds before finally pulling them out, but the grapevine disposed of them and choked them all by itself. So the weeds died and became like earth." Then Jesus continued and said, "Woe to you, for you have not learned the lesson …,that they rise from death! Blessed are you who know beforehand about what may entrap you, and who flee what is alien to you. Blessed are you who are mocked and despised because of the love your Lord has for you.

Blessed are you who weep and are afflicted by those without hope, for you will be released from all that binds you. "Watch and pray that you may not be born in the flesh, but that
you may leave the bitter bondage of this life. When you pray, you will find rest,
for you have left pain and abuse behind.

36

When you leave bodily pains and passions, you will receive rest from the Good One, and you will reign with the King, you united with the King and the King united with

you, now and forever and ever. Amen."

Parables and Saying

Several of the parables that are well-known from the canonical Gospels appear in this collection, including the parables of the sower, the rich fool, the vineyard, and the great feast. However, there is no exact parallel in the New Testament to the parable of the wise fisherman who caught a large, excellent fish and threw back all the little fish into the sea. This parable is quite different from the New Testament parable of the dragnet, but it bears a closer resemblance to the parables of the hidden treasure and the costly pearl. The Gospel of Thomas contains several parables that begin with the words "The kingdom is like," including the parables of the mustard seed, the tares, the leaven, and the lost sheep.

But the kingdom in these parables, as understood by the community to which we owe the Gospel of Thomas, is not the kingdom of the Synoptic Gospels; it is that spiritual realm to which the Gnostic is admitted by his cultivation of gnosis. Sometimes the original form of the parable has to be modified in order to make it bear this new significance.

Contrast, for example, the Synoptic parable of the stray sheep in the Gospel of Thomas:
Jesus said: 'The kingdom is like a shepherd who had a hundred sheep. One of them, the biggest, wandered away. He left the ninety-nine others and sought this single sheep until he found it. After taking this trouble, he said to the sheep: "I love you more than the ninety-nine others!"
Here the shepherd takes extra trouble over the hundredth sheep because it is the biggest one, and more valuable than all the others—probably representing the Gnostic in contrast to the many who make up the rank and file of the faithful. The parable of the costly pearl is conflated with another saying of Jesus, about laying up treasure in heaven. When the merchant has sold all his load to buy the one pearl, the admonition is added: Do you also seek for his [the Father's] imperishable treasure, which abides, where the moth does not enter and eat it up nor does the worm destroy it.

38

The parable of the hidden treasure has an uncanonical ending: when the buyer of the field had acquired the treasure, then he began to lend money at interest to whomsoever he would. This addition is probably not drawn from Matt. xxv. 27 or Luke xix. 23, where the unprofitable servant is told that he might at least have allowed his master's money to accumulate interest if he was unable or unwilling to trade with it more remuneratively. Here are two uncanonical parables of the kingdom. First comes:

Jesus said: 'The kingdom of the Father is like a woman carrying a jar full of meal and walking along a long road. The handle of the jar broke, and the meal poured out behind her on the road without her knowing it or being able to do anything about it. When she reached home, she set down the jar and found that it was empty.' This may be a warning against self-confidence, against thinking that one possesses the saving knowledge when in fact one has lost it. The kingdom of the Father is like a man who wishes to kill a magnate. In his own house he unsheathes his sword and thrusts it into the wall to make sure that his hand will be steady; then he kills his victim.

The lesson of this odd parable seems to be much the same as that of the parables of Luke xiv. 28-32; anyone who embarks upon a costly enterprise must first make sure that he has the resources to carry it out. The magnate who is attacked in the parable may further be identified with the strong man whose house is invaded and whose goods are plundered in Matthew xii. 29 and Luke xi. 21,24 the strong man being understood as the demiurge or ruler of the material order. It is unlikely that the wall into which the sword is first thrust should be allegorized.

There are sayings about fasting and circumcision which reflect a thoroughly emancipated and non-ascetic attitude towards these institutions. In such matters there were considerable differences of outlook among Gnostic sects. In the Gospel of Thomas fasting and related religious practices can be performed in a purely external manner which is positively sinful. So Saying insists: Jesus said to them: 'When you fast, you will bring sin upon yourselves; when you pray, you will be condemned; when you give alms, you will injure your spirit.

When you enter any land and go through the countryside, when you are entertained, eat what is set before you and heal the sick in those places. For nothing that enters into your mouth will defile you, but what comes out of your mouth that is what will defile you.'

The opening words about fasting, prayer and almsgiving represent a summarized reworking of Matthew vi. 1-18, and they have had appended to them passages from the commission to the seventy and Jesus' teaching about the source of real defilement.

They said: 'Come, let us pray and fast today.' Jesus said: 'What sin have I committed, or what omission am I guilty of? When the bridegroom comes forth from the bridal chamber, one never fasts or prays then.' The introduction of the bridegroom into a context where fasting is under discussion is reminiscent of Mark ii. 19 f.; but the form which Jesus' reply takes is similar to the account in the Gospel according to the Hebrews of Jesus' rejoinder to His family's suggestion that they should go and be baptized by John: 'What sin have I committed, that I should go and be baptized by him?

True fasting, however, is inculcated, as in Saying 27:

If you do not fast in relation to the world, you will not find the kingdom. If you do not make the Sabbath the (true) Sabbath, you will not see the Father. And the character of this true fasting and related religious observances is indicated in No. 6: His disciples questioned him; they said: 'Do you wish us to fast? How shall we pray and give alms and what shall we feed upon?' Jesus said: 'Tell no falsehood and do not [to others] what is hateful to yourselves; for all these things are manifest in the sight of heaven. Nothing hidden will fail to be revealed and nothing concealed will fail to be published abroad.'

With this transformation of religious obligations into ethical injunctions, we may compare the process revealed in the Western text of Acts xv. 20, 29, where the terms of the Apostolic Decree have been ethnicized and amplified by the addition of the Golden Rule (in its negative form, as here).

As for circumcision, it has no value unless it is spiritualized. According to Saying 53: His disciples said to him: 'Is circumcision useful or not?' He said to them: 'If it were useful, men's mothers would have borne them to their fathers circumcised already. But it is the true circumcision in the spirit that is profitable.'

Trinity

We cannot speak of God creating any part of himself, but God progressively reveals himself to humanity and even to himself. The Trinity is three divine persons: Father, Son, and Holy Spirit. They are not three Gods, but three divine persons who constitute one, God. The Trinity of God is a mystery that is not fully understood and is incapable of fully understanding by any human.

Godhead is an undifferentiated, unexpressed, absolute, and singular being. Godhead is the simple, essential, unified, core God. It is the necessary first and fundamental revelation of God. Every movement of God—every act of thought, will, and love—further reveals and defines God. When Godhead acts in such a way as to reveal the divine Son, Godhead reveals himself to be God the Father. God makes revelation simply by thinking or being willing. When God thinks of himself, his image, the Son of God, is revealed. The Trinity is eternal but far from static. In the Nicene creed, we read (and pray at Mass) that Christ was begotten of the Father, and the Holy Spirit proceeds from the Father and the Son. Before God was revealed as the Trinity, God was revealed as an undifferentiated Godhead.

The revelation of Godhead as the three distinct persons of the Trinity is thought to be non-optional. When Godhead thinks, he first thinks of himself (what else, no creation yet). In doing so, Godhead reveals the trait of intellect, beyond the trait of pure being of the Godhead., When Godhead thinks of himself, he generates the complete image of himself, who is the Son of God, and Godhead is now God the Father. The Son of God is the fullest expression of God. The Son of God himself is not yet fully revealed; the human children of God are called to be yet more expression of the Son of God, as the body of Christ.

The first and non-optional act of the newly revealed God the Father and God the Son is to love each other. The Father and the Son directing their wills toward each other generates the Holy Spirit. The Holy Spirit may be thought of as the bond of love (commitment) between the Father and the Son. For example, think of two people having a common pursuit; this might be marriage or a business perhaps. As this pursuit is cultivated, it becomes a real separate entity. This third entity becomes more than words. A marriage or a corporation is given a certain legal status and rights of its own. The efforts of the two people give real form to the third entity. This example is necessarily inadequate. When God thinks and wills, however, it is as real as it gets. The love of the Father and the Son toward each other is divine, selfless, full, intense, real, and permanent. Included in these thoughts is the possibility of creation outside of God. The Holy Spirit, who results, is divine, independent, full, intense, and permanent. The Holy Spirit is the acting agent of creation, sent by the Father and the Son, and is a real and complete divine person. The Holy Spirit is the result of the mutual will of the Father and the Son.

The Holy Spirit is not necessarily God's proportional will. It is possible, even likely, that the Holy Spirit is God's complete, but weighted, will, with favoritism toward mercy, joy, and peace.

Spirit

In both the canonical gospel and the Gospel of Thomas, Jesus often discusses cause and effect, the soul, and sin. These are all consequences of moral decisions and are real spiritual events. Spirit is the "mechanism" created by God for the operation of creation. Events in creation occur as a result of humanity's actions on earth, not God's manipulation from Heaven. These actions are interconnected and comprise spirit: respect, moderation, reverence, love, and hate. Like matter, the spirit is a creation of God; God is not a creation of the spirit world. What God creates is primarily spirit.

Spirit is intangible but as real as matter, and it has a real impact. It is an immaterial being that encompasses anything that exists: a rock, an idea, energy, emotion, logic, or a person. Patience, respect, hate, reverence, morality, memory, and free will are all spirits and have a real impact on our world. Spirit is the underlying framework of all creation, and the corruption of moral virtues degrades the operation of all creation.

Spirit forms matter, spirit forms spirit, and spirit forms events. Consider that anything that can be described in terms of logic, will, virtue, act, emotion, mathematics, or physical law has these same immaterial spirits or qualities as its foundation. It is commonly known that energy and matter are the same substance in different configurations. Spirit, matter, and events, likewise have an equivalence. Gospel accounts of this equivalence are the episodes in which Jesus makes bread, arms, and legs (Mt 15:31), from nothing but his will; even events may be formed; the many biblical prophecies by Jesus and others link moral action to distant future events. Immaterial acts are real, and have a real effect on our world, beginning with ourselves. "Spiritual efficacy" is the principle of the real effect of the spirit.

By definition, the spirit has no finite boundaries; will is the boundary for the spirit - God's will and man's will. Due to moral free will, virtue may be corrupted into vice. God is not the origin of evil; the abuse of virtue by moral beings is the origin of evil.

Deviation from the original perfection of God's moral design necessarily causes disorder in our world. Any deviation from perfection can only be degradation.

Although we might observe that the material world is the real and normal order of creation, the spiritual universe existed before our material world did, as with the community of the angels. This spiritual universe was no less real, and cause and effect were also real within this spiritual realm. Indeed, the world of matter is more like an overlay for the world of spirit. Spirit is the unseen framework of the entire universe, created as such by God.

The practical consequences of this are that acts of patience, moderation, justice, generosity, and chastity are real with real effects. The vices of these virtues are also real with real effect in our world. Spirit forms matter; spirit forms spirit; spirit forms events.

We must give correct attention to God, ourselves and others in all our actions. If we fail in this, the resultant act is usually weighted towards self, at the expense of God or others. Sin is a misproportion of virtue, leaving a relative lacking of some virtue.

To take the quality of respect for example; we observe that when we give undue effort to self, dignity is corrupted into arrogance. If we fail to give proper moral effort to God, then irreverence results. If we fail to give others their due, then disrespect results. In this example, if the student increased awareness of his own dignity, he would do well. But if he fails to also increase his efforts toward God's virtue of humility, then a relative lacking and resulting arrogance might result. From this, we see that moral corruption is a matter of lacking or deficit of what should be present. A lack of effort toward God leaves a relative predominance of self. The results are not theoretical, but take the forms of war, poverty, famine, and disease.

Spirit interacts directly with spirit according to common elements. The biblical ideas of a family or a nation sharing in the effects of virtue or vice are examples.

If virtue is corrupted by a person of ancient Israel (to take a common biblical example), then all who share common virtues will suffer to some degree. Persons who are of the same family, tribe, nation, or world will all feel the effects of another's good or bad actions.

This is the basis for the Biblical belief that children benefit or suffer from their parents' virtue or sin. It was true for Adam and Eve, and it is still true today. This communal nature of spirit was created by God to benefit humanity. However, with the advent of sin, the disorder was shared in addition to goodness.

God's good judgment is also a factor by which a spirit affects another spirit, matter, or events. God is incapable of creating evil, but as our parent, he does assign the evil of our sin to creation according to his good judgment. In assigning the evil created by humanity, its disorder must be felt. However, God could not assign evil with only an evil outcome possible.

A criticism of monotheism is that God seems to punish people by directing disorder (war, famine) upon them. In reality, the evil of sin generated by humanity must be affected within creation (absolute divinity cannot be corrupted). God simply assigns our evil as our parent, directing it according to his good judgment for the highest goal — the salvation of souls. It is not a matter of God punishing our bad behavior, but of God assigning our disorder. This assignment may be made directly or by extension, such as through the workings of nature. For example, 1Cor 5:5 describes our evil being affected in this life, sparing condemnation in the next.

Just as goodness may be mediated into evil, evil may be mediated into goodness. It is a matter of anger being morally mediated into patience, greed mediated into moderation and trust, and indifference into piety.

The human soul is a spirit; the soul is a "form", which gives function and purpose to one's body and actions. A human person might be thought of as a soul to which the property of physicality had been added. One's soul is the totality of one's immaterial attributes, and the operating principle of one's being.

Animals are considered to have a soul (though not immortal as in humans), which governs their operations. The human soul has traditionally been partitioned into the part that governs moral activities (superior partition or spiritual soul), the part that governs non-moral activities, and the body, (inferior partition or material soul).

It is thought that the human soul is created by God using both direct and indirect means. Those faculties of the soul which govern the body are created at conception by biological means. Those faculties of the soul having a moral dimension are thought to be created directly by God.

The human soul is not static but has the ability to "grow", and change. We may know our soul by observing our will, which in turn governs our thoughts and actions. Intellect, will, and memory are properties of our soul. Injustice and suffering in our world may only be truly eradicated by restoring its damaged spiritual foundation, which is the cause of evil. To give assistance after the fact is good, but even better is to prevent the disorder by avoiding those moral acts that degrade the spiritual foundations of our world and its people. This prevention is difficult to observe because we are attempting to observe that which is prevented.

There is not a lack of good ideas in our world, but these do not take root in hearts because of moral disorder (sin) which corrupts will, faith, brotherhood, and reasoning. War, hatred, greed, and even disease, catastrophe, and natural disasters are caused by the ongoing damage to the spiritual foundation of our world.

Hell

In the Gospel of Thomas, the idea of Heaven is more implicit, and the idea of Hell is more explicit. Heaven is full and perfected membership in Christ, who is now the entire body of Christ. Hell was never intended as a possibility since sin was never a part of the plan.

Hell is the failure of the (final) union in the body of Christ. Acting against the will of God in itself does not cast a person into Hell. Hell is unintended by the product of failed final communion. Christ's plan never included sin or even the need for salvation from Hell; what was planned was our divine communion with Christ. Jesus Christ was to have made this communion with humanity, in the absence of sin. Christ came as planned, but first had to remediate sin before his communion with humanity. Jesus Christ did not incarnate because of sin, but in spite of sin according to God's original plan.

This communion occurred as planned, but now with the introduction of sin, Hell became a possibility. What we call judgment, is this originally intended divine communion with Christ. Death was never intended and this divine communion was to have occurred in this life. In the Eucharist Christ's purpose is to make communion, and in doing so remediate (venial) sin into virtue, in order to make the communion. In baptism, Christ remediates our sin by making it into his own virtue, which also results in our communion with him.
Recall the last supper in which Jesus shared in the virtue and sin of the apostles by communion with them. That night at Gethsemane Jesus could not propagate or deflect this sin that was being presented to him.

In this communion, Christ takes goodness and those owning it, into himself. All evil and those owning it are unable to make union into Christ; what is left behind is evil (now devoid of all goodness), and those owning it. This is Hell. Purgatory is membership in the body of Christ which is short of full divine union. Those in Purgatory participate in the human nature of Christ, but not yet in his full divine nature.

This passage explains that Hell is not a punishment inflicted by God, but rather a result of a failure to achieve communion with Him. God cannot perform an act that only results in evil, and consigning someone to Hell has no possible positive outcome. Hell is instead the unintended consequence of failed communion which was planned to be perfect but corrupted by death.

Hell is created by the condemned themselves and has two degrees. The first degree is internal, occurring when a soul rejects and abandons God during a particular judgment. The result of this separation is total internal corruption. The second degree of Hell is the final Hell, which will occur at the general judgment. God will unite with all goodness in creation, taking it with Him and leaving behind what remains: undiluted evil. This Hell is what remains after God reclaims all goodness left behind by angels and humanity. The planned general communion is now the general judgment with Hell as a possibility. This general communion was Christ's desire to reunite and fulfill all of creation, that "God may be all in all", (1Cor 15:28). Everything comes from Christ, (Jn 1:3), and all is intended to rejoin Christ, even the lion who lies down with the lamb in divine Heaven.

Contextual interpretation of Jesus's sayings

Jesus said:
"Whoever cannot free themselves from their father and their mother cannot become my disciple. Whoever cannot free themselves from their brother and sister and does not bear their cross as I do is not worthy of me."

In Matthew 10:37, Jesus says that we must love Him more than our family, and in Luke 14:26, He says that we must hate our family in order to be His disciple. However, the term 'hate' is used in the sense of detachment. Love is a commitment to someone, while hate is detachment from them. Therefore, Jesus demands that we love all people, but be detached from them in order to be committed to Him. If we corrupt our love into self-seeking, it becomes lust, which we must avoid. One way to do this is by carrying our cross, as Jesus demands of us in this saying. Our salvation is to become like Christ, but we cannot do this if we remain focused on ourselves. Jesus will help us with this soul transformation, but we must do our part by detaching ourselves from self and its more vicious form, which is sin. The gospel teachings may have different wording, but they have the same core message. This is because Jesus used the same parables in His daily preaching for three years, and His wording varied.

Jesus said:
"There was a man who invited some visitors. After preparing the meal, he sent his servant to summon the guests. The servant went to the first one and said "My master invites you."
The man answered; "I have business with some merchants who are arriving this evening. Please excuse me from the dinner." The servant went to the next one and said "My master invites you."
This man answered: "I have just bought a house and need one day more, so I cannot come."

The servant went to another guest and said "My master invites you." The man answered: "My friend is getting married and I must prepare the food. Excuse me."

The servant returned to his master and said; "Those you have invited to dinner cannot come." His master replied; "Then go out on the roads and invite whoever you find to dine with me. Buyers and merchants will not enter my Father's dwelling."

From Lk 14:16, "Then Jesus said to him, 'A man gave agave a great dinner and invited many. At the time for the dinner he sent his slave to say to those who had been invited,

'Come; for everything is ready now.' But they all alike began to make excuses. The first said to him, 'I have bought a piece of land, and I must go out and see it; please accept my regrets.' Another said, 'I have bought five yoke of oxen, and I am going to try them out; please accept my regrets.'

Another said, 'I have just been married, and therefore I cannot come.' So the slave returned and reported this to his master. Then the owner of the house became angry and said to his slave, 'Go out at once into the streets and lanes of the town and bring in the poor, the crippled, the blind, and the lame.' And the slave said, 'Sir, what you ordered has been done, and there is still room." Then the master said to the slave, 'Go out into the roads and lanes, and compel people to come in, so that my house may be filled. For I tell you, none of those who were invited will taste my dinner.'"

In both the canonical and Gospel of Thomas, Jesus speaks in hyperbole or exaggeration. Virtually no one could be saved if God were only strict justice. Look at the last paragraph in Thomas, "Buyers and merchants will not enter the places of my Father.". This sound bite in isolation would be considered at variance with Catholic teaching. The sayings of the Gospel of Thomas are far more isolated than the canonical gospels, and we must acknowledge this as we study it. We could even isolate the canonical gospels to the point of error, and it has been done.

It is interesting that the slaves mentioned are the prophets of God, who invite others to union with God. Here, a slave is not a disgruntled prisoner, but a pure instrument of God's will.

Jesus said:

"Those who know the All yet do not know themselves are deprived of everything.

God is the All, and if we believe that God is anything less than eternal, absolute, and complete; then we are lacking in knowledge of God. Our incomplete knowledge of God is a symptom of our incomplete participation in God."

Regarding Gnosticism, it is unlikely that someone would have forged this text as it does not support the idea of multiple gods, which is central to Gnosticism. The Gospel of Thomas does not contain any sayings that explicitly endorse Gnosticism. While it is possible to interpret the teachings of Jesus in a way that aligns with Gnostic beliefs, this is not done in the Gospel of Thomas, which is consistent with mainstream Christian teaching.

The Gospel of Thomas emphasizes that true value lies not in material possessions but in the state of our souls. Knowledge without inner transformation is meaningless. Job, a figure from the Hebrew Bible, once said to God, "I knew you only by hearsay. Now I know you in my flesh; my eyes have seen you!" To move from hearsay to realization is to move from words and beliefs to action and wholeness.

The self-knowledge that is central to the Gospel of Thomas is not about self-analysis or narcissistic introspection. It involves observing our reactions and emotions without judgment, which allows us to understand who we truly are.

Jesus said:

"The harvest is abundant, but the workers are few. Pray for the Master to send more workers to the harvest."

This is a virtual retelling of Mt 9:37-38. The workers dispatched for the harvest or bringing in of souls are Christians who are literally Christ in our world.

They continue his redemptive mission by giving the sacraments, and most vitally by the remediation of sin into virtue, allowing the incorporation of the individual into the perfect person of Christ.

The Master said:
"There are many who stand around the well, but no one to go down into it."

This is clearly not spoken by Jesus, but to Jesus. It could mean many things. Perhaps there is a dry well that Jesus miraculously fills. Jesus also repeatedly taught that the Law of Moses itself could not save; perhaps a Pharisee comes to this knowledge and states this in figurative speech.

The Law of Moses went far toward salvation, but the final and vital element of salvation is an actual sharing in the person of Jesus Christ. To stop at the Law of Moses would be akin to people looking at an empty trough, which only the Messiah may fill.

Jesus said:
"Many are standing by the door, but only those who are alone and simple can enter the bridal chamber."

This is related to Luke 14:26, "If anyone comes to me without hating his father and mother, wife and children. Those who are alone may devote their will entirely to Christ when their will is fulfilled; they become members of Christ, who is now the entire body of Christ.

In fact, we must love all others which means that we are committed in a will to them. Literal aloneness is not demanded once we go beyond this isolated verse. In the beatitudes (Matthew 5:1-12), Jesus does not demand actual poverty, but 'poverty in spirit', this is a matter of not desiring wealth, rather than not having wealth.

We might substitute the word "one" for "alone". Now those who are one (the single person of Christ, who is now the entire body of Christ) may enter Heaven, who is the very person of Christ.

Jesus said:

"I am the Light that shines on everyone. I am the All. The All came forth from me and the All came into me. Split the wood, and I am there. Turn over the stone, and there you will find me."

The first paragraph combines the gospel ideas of John 1:3 (all things came into being through Jesus), and Rev 22:13, ("I am the Alpha and the Omega, the first and the last, the beginning and the end.").

The second and third paragraphs are not about pantheism (God is all things), but divine omnipresence (God is in all things). At a minimum Christ's attribute of existing in all things. If something did not have the attribute of being, it would not exist or cease to exist. This attribute of being may be given by extended means, but it must have its origin and its own ongoing existence in God. If God ceased to think of something or ceased to will it, it would cease to be. God not only knows everything (divine omniscience), but God has a presence in everything and sustains everything, which we call divine omnipresence.

St. Thomas Aquinas dismissed this idea and argued that God has a non-moral presence even in demons. According to Aquinas, demons were created as angels with the attribute of being, and as devils, they still possess this non-moral attribute of being. If not, they would cease to exist.

When Yeshua says "I am the All," he means that he embodies the integration of all polarities and opposites. He represents the union of the human and the divine, the finite and the infinite, time and eternity.

Christ takes on all human faces; none of them are foreign to him. He has shown the face of human transfiguration and disfiguration, and has played the roles of sage, slave, and sacrificial lamb. He embodies both the brightest light and the deepest darkness, suffering, and beatitude. He has experienced all stages of human existence, including death.

Thus when he says "I am the All," he does not mean some outer (and rather vague) totality, but rather the power of integration of all polarities contained in humanity and in the cosmos, or pleroma (a Greek word, sometimes translated as "fullness" and often used by gnostics, as well as by Paul and John in the canonical gospels). Nothing is to be excluded, but everything is to be transfigured, and integrated—even the absurd, evil, and death. This is shown in the story of Christ.

In psychological terms, we may say that Christ is alive in us when we are totally ourselves, excluding nothing of what we are.

Jesus said:

"Why do you roam the countryside? To see some reeds shaken by the wind? To see people like your kings and courtiers in elegant clothes? They wear fine clothes, but they cannot know the truth."

Mt 11:7-9, "As they went away, Jesus began to speak to the crowds about John: 'What did you go out into the wilderness to look at? A reed shaken by the wind? What then did you go out to see? Someone dressed in soft robes? Look, those who wear soft robes are in royal palaces. What then did you go out to see? A prophet? Yes, I tell you, and more than a prophet.'"

Jesus is speaking about John the Baptist. As to the last sentence, it is the established teaching that indulgence of self, prohibits by degree a deeper sharing outside of self, in the person of Christ.

Jesus said:

"When images become visible to people, the light that is in them is hidden. In the icon of the light of the Father, it will be manifest and the icon veiled by the light."

Start with, "The light within them (Jesus Christ), is in the image of the Father", (Jesus is the image of the Father). "He (the Father) will be disclosed" (in Heaven), "But (for now) his image is hidden by his light", (his light or image is Jesus).

The Letter to the Colossians is even more explicit: "He is the image of the invisible God, first-born of all creatures, for it is in him that all things are created in heaven and on earth, visible and invisible […] He is before all things, and all things subsist in him."

This is an Icon that, rather than hiding the light as ordinary images do, is itself hidden by the light, which envelops it totally. The revelation of Christ, far from putting an end to the Mystery, only deepens it.

Jesus said:

"When you see your true likeness, you rejoice. But when you see your icons, those that were before you existed, and that never dies and never manifest, what grandeur! We are an eternal idea within God. When we are given creation, the (perfect) idea of us within God does not cease. "

Perhaps in Heaven, we will be given knowledge of God's perfect idea of us, it could be a lot to bear. This ideal would be compared to our actual spiritual attainment. The Marian apparition of Garabandal alludes to a worldwide revelation of consciousness, which may be similar. Perhaps Jesus is referring to such a personal revelation at the death of each of us.

Jesus said:

"Adam was produced by a great power and a great wealth, yet he was not worthy of you. If he had been worthy, he would not have known death."

This is Jesus speaking to disciple Christians who are saved and share in the body of Christ. Strictly speaking this participation in the body of Christ, first occurred at the Eucharist of the last supper, but Jesus does not discourage the good news with details of sequence. At times Jesus disregarded the salvation sequence in the canonical gospels. Adam, even in his pre-sinful state did not enjoy stature as a member of Christ (the body of Christ), and is, therefore, lesser than a member of Christ.

This is similar to the teaching in Mt 11:11, that the least in the divine kingdom of Heaven is greater than the great human prophet John the Baptist.

56

Again the Catholic teaching on membership in the body of Christ is that we first share in the human nature of Jesus Christ, (which explains why we do walk around divine); then in Heaven, we share in the full divine nature of Christ. Adam was a man of light until he tasted the fruit of the Tree of Knowledge of Good and Evil, the tree of dualistic and subjective knowledge ("What makes me happy I call good, what makes me unhappy I call evil"). It could also be described as the tree of egocentric knowledge. To eat of its mortal fruit is to elevate the small self, the ego, to the status of critic and judge of what is good and bad. Gnosis is the surrender of this form of egocentric, "mortal" knowledge to the theocentric, or nondual, knowledge of the Tree of Life. As St. John of the Cross said, "May I know all things from God, not from myself; for I can know only an effect from its cause, never a cause from its effect." Then the critical or judging aspect, with its memories, desires, and fears, ceases to reside in our personality. Only God, the divine Self, can accomplish this. It is then that we cease to eat the mortal fruit and take nourishment instead from the Living One in all things.

Jesus said:
"Foxes have their holes and birds have their nests. The Son of Man has no place to lay his head and rest."

From Mt 8:20, "And Jesus said to him, "Foxes have holes, and birds of the air have nests; but the Son of Man has nowhere to lay his head."

Jesus said:
"Wretched is the body that depends on another body. Wretched is the soul that depends on both. The body which depends only upon itself and has not dependence or sharing in God is miserable."

The body that depends on a body refers to a person that relies only upon this world. A soul that limits its participation to the two bodies spoken of in the first part is even that much more miserable. Our soul is to share in Christ, rather than limit itself to this world.

Jesus said:

"Angels and prophets will come to you and give you what is yours. And you, too, should give what you have and ask yourselves; When will the time come for them to take what is theirs?"

This saying from Jesus in the Gospel of Thomas highlights the idea of reciprocity in spiritual relationships. Angels and prophets are understood as messengers of God who come to deliver messages and guidance to humans. In return, humans are expected to give what they have, both materially and spiritually, to others and to God.

The idea of giving what one has is also linked to the concept of stewardship, which is a key theme in Christianity. Christians believe that they are stewards of God's creation and are responsible for taking care of the earth and all its inhabitants. This includes sharing their resources and talents with others and working towards social justice and equality.

The second part of the saying suggests that there will come a time when angels and prophets will take what is theirs. This could be interpreted as a warning that there will come a time of judgment when humans will be held accountable for their actions and will be required to give an account of their stewardship.

Overall, this saying emphasizes the importance of reciprocity, stewardship, and accountability in spiritual relationships. It encourages believers to be generous with their resources and to work towards building a just and equitable society.

They said to him:

"Tell us who you are so that we may believe in you." He answered them: You search the face of heaven and earth, but you do not recognize the one who is in your presence and you do not know how to experience the present moment.

Many disciples were slow to acknowledge Jesus as Christ the Messiah. In fairness, the first paragraph shows prudent caution, as in Israel there was always someone claiming to be Messiah.

"...why do you not know how to interpret the present time?" The present time was a time of special grace, with Jesus in the world for only a few years. Now was the time for Israel to make its prophesied fulfillment in the Messiah. Jesus said:

Seek and you shall find. Yet those things you asked me about before and which I did not tell you

I am willing to reveal now, but you no longer ask.

"Ask, and it will be given you; search, and you will find; knock, and the door will be opened for you." From the second paragraph, we learn that Jesus did not reveal all the mysteries of God, salvation and the future at once. His prophecy of the destruction of the temple, the tribulation, and his own death all came later. His theology of the Eucharist was revealed halfway through his ministry, and many left him. This event may have occurred near the end of his ministry, and he wanted to complete his teachings.

Do not give sacred things to dogs, for they may treat them as dung. Do not throw pearls to swine, for they may treat them as rubbish.

Whoever seeks will find; whoever knocks from inside, it will open to them. If you have money, do not lend it with interest, but give it to the one who will never pay you back.

The Kingdom of the Father is like the dough in which a woman has hidden some yeast. It becomes transformed into good bread. Those who have ears let them hear!

The creative Intelligence, that tiny seed of infinity, is at work within us. It is that which urges and leads us on, from the state of flour or shapeless dough to that of good, well-baked bread.

But the dough also needs time to rise and must be kneaded by the woman—Sophia, or Wisdom—before it will be ready to be transformed by the divine Fire.

This is the fulfillment of the mission of the seed of light within us.

The Kingdom of the Father is like the woman who carried a jar of flour.

After she walked a long way, the handle of the jar broke and the flour began to spill behind her along the road. Heedless, she noticed nothing. When she arrived, she set down the jar and found it empty.

This is a warning parable, similar to "He replied, 'I tell you that to everyone who has, more will be given, but as for the one who has nothing, even what they have will be taken away.'" It is similar also to the Gospel of Thomas saying.

The theology is as follows: What we call judgment is actually God's originally intended communion with a person. Christ makes the communion, rejoining all goodness to himself, all evil and those owning it will be unable to make the communion, and the evil left behind is Hell. From this saying and the gospel verses we see that it is possible that "even what we think we have, will be taken from us." See also the appendix for an explanation of the process of Hell.

The Kingdom of the Father is like the man who wanted to kill a man of power. First, he unsheathed his sword at home and thrust it into the wall to test his strength. Then he answered and said to them, "Those here who do the will of my Father are my brothers and my mother. It is they who will enter the Kingdom of my Father."

This statement can be found in Matthew 12:48-50, and it emphasizes the importance of following God's will. Jesus is not diminishing the significance of his family, but he is stating that spiritual family is just as important as a biological family. By doing God's will, we become a part of a greater family, united by our faith and love for God.

They showed Jesus a gold coin and said to him:
"Caesar's agents demand that we pay taxes."
He answered them; Give to Caesar what is Caesar's, gives to God what is God's, and give to me what is mine.

Jesus said:

"Whoever does not hate their father and mother as I do cannot become my disciple. And whoever does not love their father and mother as I do cannot become my disciple. For my mother made me to die, but my true mother gave me Life."

This is a virtual retelling of Mt 12:46-50, "While he was still speaking to the crowds, his mother and his brothers were standing outside, wanting to speak to him. Someone told him, 'Look, your mother and your brothers are standing outside, wanting to speak to you.' But to the one who had told him this, Jesus replied, 'Who is my mother, and who are my brothers?' And pointing to his disciples, he said, 'Here are my mother and my brothers! For whoever does the will of my Father in heaven is my brother and sister and mother.'" We might rephrase the last sentence, "Whoever does the will of the Father, is now rejoined to me as the body of Christ, and they will not lose their former human office, but will gain divine nature."

In the body of Christ, we will not lose our attributes of: brother sister, and mother. Since we will all share in one another (Rm 12:5), the mother of one member is the mother of all members, including Jesus who is the preeminent member of the body of Christ.

The emphasis here is on loving—and refusing to love—as Yeshua does.

We love our mother and father for what they are, but we do not love their tendencies to perpetuate a web of neurotic codependency. Such a relationship makes us oblivious to our second birth and to the true mother who engendered us not to die, but to know true life.

In Hebrew the word ruah, translated as "spirit" or "breath," is feminine. In the context of a patriarchal society, Yeshua dared to offer privileged revelations to women (to Mary Magdalene and to the Samaritan woman, for example), and his gnostic successors emphasized the feminine gender of ruah in an effort to restore the rightful place of the feminine and maternal aspect of Divinity.

Of course, God, the Uncreated beyond all images, is neither masculine nor feminine. But it is important to have a balance in the symbols we use in trying to speak of the Unnamable. This is why Sophia, who is Wisdom and also the Divine Mother, has such an important place in gnostic texts.

In the Acts of Thomas, the name Mother is used to invoke the Spirit. In Manichean writings, she is often called Mother of Life, and in the Gospel of Philip, it is said that Adam received the Breath from his mother.

Jesus said:
"Wretched are the Pharisees. They are like the dog lying in the cow's manger. He cannot eat, and will not let the cows eat."

Similar to Mt 23:13, "Woe to you, teachers of the law and Pharisees, you hypocrites! You shut the door of the kingdom of heaven in people's faces. You yourselves do not enter, nor will you let those enter who are trying to."

The Pharisees were self-indulgent in prideful perfection of piety, and criticism of others. They did not enter the kingdom of Heaven, and they said that those less perfect in ritual piety would not enter Heaven.

Jesus said:
"The heavens and the earth will roll up before you. The living who come from the Living will know neither fear nor death, for it is said: Whoever has self-knowledge, the world cannot contain them."

Isaiah 66:22 and 2 Peter 3:13 both speak of a new Heaven and a new earth. Here Jesus refers to Heaven as being created by God (angels, thrones, dominions). All of Heaven and earth are intended to have final fulfillment as part of divine Christ, God will be "all in all things", (1 Corinthians 15:28). In this saying, we are not the cause of this, but observers of it.
The second paragraph is a retelling of saying 56. Jesus may have made this teaching repeatedly in his mission. Here the speaker is likely the apostle Thomas, who is the recorder of the Gospel of Thomas.

Jesus said:
"Wretched is the flesh that depends on the soul; wretched is the soul that depends on the flesh."

Our bodies have been given over to the corruption of sin; we all have physical death. The 'flesh' in the saying is under a certain curse of death. In the second sentence, the soul that does not participate beyond the flesh (into Christ) is also under a curse of spiritual death.

The disciples asked him:
"When will the Kingdom come?"
Jesus answered:
"It will not come by watching for it. No one will be saying, Look, here it is! Alternatively, look, there it is! The Kingdom of the Father is spread out over the whole earth, and people do not see it."

Similar to saying three. Jesus tells the disciples that the prophesied kingdom of God will not be a new government or temple, it is here already, and it is he. In saying that the kingdom of Heaven is spread out upon the earth, Jesus may be comparing his own humble mission, to the widely anticipated and glorious new Messiah-king of Israel, or to some extraordinary or cosmic event.

Simon Peter said to him:
"Mary should leave us, for women are not worthy of Life."
Jesus answered:
"This is how I will guide her so that she becomes Man. She, too, will become a living breath like you Men. Any woman who makes herself a Man will enter into the Kingdom of God."

The first paragraph is not a teaching of Jesus; it is an emotional explosion of Peter. The author acknowledges Peter as the best of men, but Peter did make moral mistakes.
This saying is another mistaken act of Peter. It is embarrassing but likely true.

By true or false legend, Mary Magdalene was a notorious prostitute possessed by seven devils, (and just the kind of person Jesus loved). Perhaps Mary applies as a disciple and Peter loudly objects.

If Peter's denial of Jesus had not appeared in the canonical gospel, but only in the Gospel of Thomas, we would declare it inauthentic, even though it did in fact happen.

So this saying in the Gospel of Thomas is entirely possible. In this Gospel of Thomas saying, Peter is likely speaking of Mary Magdalene. Jesus soundly corrects Peter, "LOOK! I will guide her to make her male…" We are to share in the very person of the man Jesus. The larger truth of the body of Christ is that "There is neither Jew nor Gentile, neither slave nor free, nor is there male and female, for you are all one in Christ Jesus.", (Galatians 3:28).

The body of Christ is now all who share in the life and person of the Son of God: Jesus, angels, Eucharist, and humans. They all make up the single person

Biblical text Abbreviations

I Cor, II Cor First Corinthians, Second Corinthians
I John First Letter of John
I Peter First Letter of Peter
I Thess, II Thess First Thessalonians, Second Thessalonians
I Tim First Timothy
Col Colossians
Dan Daniel
Deut Deuteronomy
Eccus Ecclesiasticus/Sirach
Eph Ephesians
Ex Exodus
Ezek Ezekiel
Gal Galatians
Gen Genesis
Heb Hebrews
James Epistle of James
Jer Jeremiah
John The Gospel of John
Lev Leviticus
Luke The Gospel of Luke
Mark The Gospel of Mark
Matt The Gospel of Matthew
Num Numbers
Phil Philippians
Prov Proverbs
Rev Revelation
Rom Romans
Zach Zachariah

The Gospel of Mary Magdalene - The First Apostle Woman

Introduction

Most people today are not familiar with the Gospel of Mary. It was written in the early second century CE, but disappeared for over 1,500 years until a single, incomplete translation in Coptic surfaced in the late 1800s. We do not know how it was found, but we do know that the manuscript that contained it was bought by Carl Reinhardt in Cairo and taken to Berlin in 1896. More fragments in Greek were found in the 1900s, but a complete copy of the Gospel of Mary has not been found yet. Only about eight pages of the ancient text remain, so around half of it might be lost forever.

Despite its short length, these few pages offer an interesting look into a form of Christianity that was forgotten for a long time. This short account presents a different interpretation of Jesus' teachings as a way to gain internal spiritual knowledge. It rejects the idea that his suffering and death were the way to eternal life. It shows that the idea that Mary of Magdala was a harlot is a made-up story. It argues that women can be leaders, which is rare in early Christian writing. It criticizes corrupt authority and imagines a world where we strive for spiritual excellence. It challenges our idealized views of the unity and harmony of the first Christians. It makes us reconsider the foundation of church power. And all of this was written in the name of a woman.

The story of the Gospel of Mary is simple. As the first six pages are missing, the gospel starts in the middle of a conversation between the Savior and his disciples after his resurrection. The Savior answers their questions about the end of the physical world and sin. He teaches them that everything, whether material or spiritual, is connected. This will not be true in the end. Everything will go back to its own origin and fate.

However, for now, sin is related to life in this mixed world. People sin because they do not recognize their own spiritual nature and instead value their lower nature, which misleads them and leads to illness and death. Salvation is achieved by finding the genuinely spiritual nature of humanity within oneself and overcoming physical passions and the world.

The Savior ends this lesson with a warning against those who might deceive the disciples into following a heroic leader or a set of rules. Instead, they should look inside themselves and find inner peace. After telling them to spread the gospel, the Savior leaves.

But the disciples do not go out joyfully to preach the gospel; instead, controversy erupts. All the disciples except Mary have failed to comprehend the Savior's teaching. Rather than seek peace within, they are distraught, frightened that if they follow his commission to preach the gospel, they might share his agonizing fate. Mary steps in and comforts them and, at Peter's request, relates teaching unknown to them that she had received from the Savior in a vision. The Savior had explained to her the nature of prophecy and the rise of the soul to its final rest, describing how to win the battle against the wicked, illegitimate powers that seek to keep the soul entrapped in the world and ignorant of its true spiritual nature.

But as she finishes her account, two of the disciples quite unexpectedly challenge her. Andrew objects that her teaching is strange and he refuses to believe that it came from the Savior. Peter goes further, denying that Jesus would ever have given this kind of advanced teaching to a woman, or that Jesus could possibly have preferred her to them. Apparently, when he asked her to speak, Peter had not expected such elevated teaching, and now he questions her character, implying that she has lied about having received special teaching in order to increase her stature among the disciples.

Severely taken aback, Mary begins to cry at Peter's accusation. Levi comes quickly to her defense, pointing out to Peter that he is a notorious hothead and now he is treating Mary as though she were the enemy.

"We should be ashamed of ourselves," he admonishes them all; "instead of arguing among ourselves, we should go out and preach the gospel as the Savior commanded us."

The story ends here, but the controversy is far from resolved. Andrew and Peter, at least, and likely the other fearful disciples as well, have not understood the Savior's teaching and are offended by Jesus' apparent preference of a woman over them. Their limited understanding and false pride make it impossible for them to comprehend the truth of the Savior's teaching. The reader must both wonder and worry what kind of gospel such proud and ignorant disciples will preach.

How can we understand this story? It seems similar to the gospels of the New Testament, but there are also differences. The characters are familiar, like Jesus, Mary, Peter, Andrew, and Levi. They talk about the gospel and the kingdom of God, and Jesus says things like "Those who seek will find" and "Anyone with two ears should listen." In the New Testament, Jesus appears to his disciples after the resurrection, and this happens in the Gospel of Mary too. But there are also some significant differences. For example, after Jesus commissions the disciples, they don't go out to preach the gospel as they do in Matthew. Instead, they weep, afraid for their lives. Some of the things Jesus says might shock modern readers, like when he says there is no such thing as sin. Andrew thinks these teachings are strange ideas.

The Gospel of Mary was written when Christianity was new and small. There were many Christian communities spread around the Eastern Mediterranean, and they were often isolated from each other. They were small enough to meet in someone's home without attracting too much attention. At first, Christians relied on oral practices like preaching, teaching, and rituals of table fellowship and baptism. Written documents were not as important. They were only used as guides to preaching and practice. We can't assume that all the churches had the same documents.

The people who wrote the first Christian literature lost most of it. Christoph Markschies thinks we have lost 85% of Christian literature from the first two centuries, and that's only the literature we know about. There must be even more because the discovery of texts like the Gospel of Mary was a surprise.

We can't reconstruct the whole of early Christian history and practice from the few surviving texts. Our picture will always be incomplete, not only because so much is lost but because early Christian practices were not tied to writing.

As a result of their distinct development and unique situations, these early churches often had divergent perspectives on key aspects of Christian doctrine and practice. Fundamental questions, such as the meaning and substance of Jesus' teachings, the nature of salvation, the authority of prophets, and the roles of women and slaves, were hotly debated. Early Christians put forth and tested competing models of the ideal community.

It is crucial to keep in mind that these first Christians did not possess a New Testament, the Nicene Creed or Apostles Creed, a universally agreed upon church hierarchy or order, church buildings, and indeed, no single view of Jesus. The elements that we might consider to be indispensable to define Christianity were nonexistent at the time. The Nicene Creed and the New Testament were the end products of these disputes and debates, rather than starting points. They symbolize the distillation of experience and experimentation, and not a negligible amount of conflict and strife.

All early Christian literature reflects these controversies. The earliest extant Christian documents, the letters of Paul, show that significant differences of opinion existed regarding issues such as circumcision, Jewish dietary laws, or the relative importance of spiritual gifts. These and other contentious topics, such as whether the resurrection was physical or spiritual, sparked theological debates and caused divisions within and between Christian communities. By the time of the Gospel of Mary, these conversations were becoming increasingly nuanced and polarized.

As we know, history is written by the victors. In the context of early Christianity, this meant that many voices in these discussions were silenced through suppression or neglect.

The Gospel of Mary, along with other recently unearthed works from the earliest days of Christianity, broadens our understanding of the tremendous variety and dynamic nature of the procedures that shaped Christianity. The objective of this volume is to enable twenty-first-century readers to hear one of those voices—not to silence the voices of canon and tradition, but to make them more audible, thanks to an expanded historical perspective. Whether or not readers choose to accept the message of the Gospel of Mary is a decision they must make for themselves.

Dialogue, Message and teachings in the Gospel

The appearances of Jesus after his resurrection are recorded in all four of the New Testament gospels and Acts, as well as in other early Christian writings such as the First Apocalypse of James and the Dialogue of the Savior. These appearances serve to confirm the reality of Jesus' resurrection, and they primarily portray the post-resurrection period as a time when Jesus imparted special teachings and commissioned his disciples to preach the gospel. The appearance of the risen Lord, the rebuke of fearful or grieving disciples, the association of special teachings with the risen Lord, the disciples as the recipients of the teachings, the mention of opponents, persecution for holding secret teachings, and a commissioning scene are all typical post-resurrection scenes.

The Savior's teachings are also heavily emphasized in the Gospel of Mary, whether in his own words or through Mary's account of the revelation to her. Although the title of the book identifies it as a "gospel," which is commonly associated with a story of Jesus' life and teachings, it meant the "good news" of the kingdom to the earliest Christians, which indicated the message and promise of the Savior rather than the genre of the work. The Gospel of Mary structured as a series of dialogues and departures, better fits the formal conventions of a post-resurrection dialogue.

These dialogues not only communicate the content of the Gospel of Mary, but they also emphasize the dialogical character of its teachings. The messages are amplified by the work's structure, which draws the reader deeper inward. The structural similarity between the two main dialogues authorizes Mary's teaching and her leadership role by placing her in a position parallel to that of the Savior. In this way, the structure of the Gospel of Mary reproduces the same message as the Savior's teaching: "Acquire my peace within yourselves... For the child of true Humanity exists within you. Follow it! Those who seek for it will find it."

Both the Savior and Mary serve as teachers in the Gospel of Mary. While the Savior answers his followers' questions, Mary shares her conversation with him. Because it requires active participation from the student, dialogue is the primary mode of instruction. The Savior's goal is to instill proper attitudes in his disciples, such as warning them not to be afraid of the dangers ahead and praising Mary for remaining calm when she saw him. By doing so, he hopes to bring his disciples up to, if not surpass, his level of understanding. After his departure, Mary is able to take his place, demonstrating the success of the Savior's teachings.

Dialogical pedagogy acknowledges the teacher's higher status but believes that this distinction is temporary and should disappear as the student progresses. To achieve freedom and efficacy, the disciples must appropriate the truth of the Savior's teachings for themselves. The Savior warns them not to rely on external authority and encourages them to look within themselves because the child of true Humanity exists within them. They can achieve a level of understanding that frees them from domination by discovering the truth for themselves.

The Possessed

And there were some females who had been cured of evil spirits and illnesses, including Mary, also known as Magdalene, who had been freed from seven demons, Joanna, the wife of Khuza (a commissioner of Herod), Susanna, and many others who supported them with their possessions.

Mary makes her first appearance in the chronology of Jesus' life in this brief passage from Luke's Gospel (8:2-3), which shows when she entered Jesus' life and why she sought him out. Jesus' reputation must have attracted her to travel the difficult ten miles from her home in Magdala to Capernaum, where he lived from 24 C.E. until the early part of 27 C.E. It's possible she came to him on foot, over rocky roads and rough paths, possessed by demons and dressed in rags. According to estimates, she sought him out in 25 C.E., after Jesus had become known in Galilee as a rabbi who welcomed sinners and fought demons that afflicted them. Although there is no evidence that Jesus visited Magdala before 25 C.E., he may have done so.

If she had started her journey from Magdala with a woolen cloak, which was desirable among travelers for shelter at night as well as coverage in rain and cold, it and any leather sandals she wore might have been stolen. However, cloaks and sandals were not affordable for every family, and the poor had to make their way barefoot, warmed only by the thick flax of their tunics. The toughness of these Galilean peasants, who spent their days outdoors even in the cold winter rains and occasional snow of the region, can only be imagined.

Luke's portrayal of Mary is not that of the wealthy and elegant temptress of medieval legend and modern fantasy. One vivid story, told and embellished in the sixth century in the Asia Minor city of Ephesus, portrays Mary as so wealthy that she was invited to a dinner with Tiberius Caesar in Rome after Jesus' death. She used the occasion to preach about Jesus' Resurrection, only to be met with imperial mockery.

The emperor stated that God would not raise the dead any more than he would change the color of the egg in Mary's hand from white to red. According to the story, the egg immediately turned red. Orthodox Christians still recount this story at Easter, and Mary and her egg are depicted in the icons of Eastern Orthodoxy.

Some contemporary scholarship has attempted to support the notion of Mary's wealth by emphasizing her association with Joanna in Luke's Gospel since Joanna had married into the prominent household of Herod Antipas, the ruler of Galilee. In one recent reconstruction, Mary and the influential Joanna were friends and business partners; Mary used Joanna's contacts and her own wealth to host dinner parties at which she employed Jesus as a comedian. Revisionist readings, like medieval legends, can stimulate and refresh our imaginations, but they also demonstrate how much the Western religious imagination desires a rich and powerful Mary to protect the poor and defenseless Jesus.

However, Luke's Gospel does not claim that Mary had the same status as Joanna; rather, it distinguishes between the two women. Joanna, who was married to a government official and was aristocratic, possibly wealthy, and well-connected, was one of the women mentioned by Luke. Mary, on the other hand, lacked Joanna's social standing and connections. Instead, she was possessed by demons. There is no evidence in ancient texts (or reasonable speculation) that Jesus ever lived in Magdala or that Mary owned property there that she gave to Jesus to use. Mary's story is not limited to her encounter with Jesus. She also plays a prominent role in the Gospel accounts of Jesus' crucifixion and resurrection. According to the Gospel of John, Mary was present at the foot of the cross with Jesus' mother and other women, while the other Gospels mention her among the women who went to the tomb on the morning of the third day after Jesus' death to anoint his body with spices.

Mary is the first person to see the risen Jesus in the Gospel of John, and he appears to her alone.

This encounter marks a turning point in the Gospel, as Mary transitions from mourning the loss of her beloved teacher to proclaiming to the other disciples the good news of his resurrection. Throughout the centuries, artists, writers, and theologians have been captivated by Mary Magdalene's story. Some traditions regard her as a repentant sinner who found redemption through her encounter with Jesus, while others regard her as a saint and a model of faith and devotion. Regardless of how one interprets her story, Mary Magdalene remains an important figure in the Christian tradition and a powerful symbol of hope, transformation, and the enduring power of love.

Given Mary's demonic possession, there is little mystery about her being single. Possession carried the stigma of impurity, not the natural impurity of childbirth (for example), but the contagion of an unclean spirit. She had no doubt been ostracized in Magdala in view of her many demons. The Jews of Galilee defined themselves, in contrast to the Gentiles around them, by their devotion to stringent laws of purity that were commanded by the Torah, the Law of Moses that was written in Hebrew and passed on in oral form in the Aramaic language. What they ate, whom they could eat and associate with, how they farmed, whom they could touch or not touch, the people they could marry, the kind of sex they had and when they had it— all this and more was determined by this Torah. The Galileans' purity was their identity, more precious and delightful in their minds than prosperity under the Romans or even survival. They resorted to violent resistance sporadically during the first century to expunge the impurity the Romans had brought to their land, even when that resistance proved suicidal.

"Unclean spirits," as Jesus and his followers often called demons, inhabited Mary. These demons were considered contagious, moving from person to person and place to place, transmitted by people like Mary who were known to be possessed. In the Hellenistic world, an invisible contagion of this kind was called a daimon, the origin of the word demon. But a daimon needn't be harmful in the sources of Greco-Roman thought.

Demons hovered in the space between the terrestrial world and the realm of the gods. When Socrates was asked how he knew how to act when he faced an ethical dilemma, he said that he listened to his daimonion ti, a nameless "little daimon" that guided him.

Judaism during this period referred to the same kind of forces, using the language of spirit and distinguishing between good spirits (such as angels and the Holy Spirit that God breathed over the world) and bad spirits. Jesus called harmful spiritual influences "unclean" or "evil" spirits, and the word daimon has been used in this sense within both Judaism and Christianity. After all, even a "good" daimon from the Hellenistic world was associated with idolatry, and that is why the term demon is used in a pejorative sense in modern languages influenced by Church practices. Everyone in the ancient world, Jewish or not, agreed that demons could do harm, invading people, animals, and objects, inhabiting and possessing them. While demons are in some ways comparable to psychological complexes, they are also analogous to our bacteria, viruses, and microbes.

People protected themselves from invisible demons with the care we devote to hygiene, and ancient experts listed them the way we catalog diseases and their alleged causes. Such lists have survived on fragments of papyrus that record the ancient craft of exorcism. The fact that these experts disagreed did not undermine belief in demons any more than changing health advice today makes people skeptical of science. Then, as now, conflict among experts only heightened belief in the vital importance of the subject.

Some scholars have argued that women in early Greece were thought more susceptible of possession than men, on the dubious grounds that their vaginas made their bodies vulnerable to entry. Ancient thought was usually subtler than that, and demons do not seem to have required many apertures or much room for maneuver.

A person's eyes, ears, and nose were much more likely to expose him to their influences than any orifice below the waist. However Mary came by her demons, they rendered her unclean within the society of Jewish Galilee. She was probably very much alone when she arrived in Capernaum.

In ancient times, women who lacked family were vulnerable in ways that are difficult to fathom. The Gospels usually referred to women as sisters, wives, or mothers of men, and this connection served as their protection. As was the case in many cultures, if a married woman was alone with any man other than her husband in a private place, she could be accused of adultery (Sotah 1:1-7 Mishnah, a Rabbinic tradition that applied the Law of Moses). Similarly, a man who stayed in his future father-in-law's home could not claim later that his wife was not a virgin, as he might have had sex with her given the chance. Women without men did not make themselves available; rather, men took advantage of them.

Upon reaching puberty, a young woman transitioned from her father's custody to that of her husband. Weddings were arranged between families for mutual benefit, such as increasing their families, fields, herds, labor force, and trade connections. Marriage was a binding contract that was recorded in writing in literate communities or witnessed in illiterate peasant communities. After the marriage contract was agreed upon, a young woman stayed in her father's home for a year or so. However, even with this delay of sexual relations, pregnant fourteen- and fifteen-year-old women must have been a relatively common sight.

This arrangement was designed to preserve Israel's bloodlines' purity by managing a woman's transition from puberty to childbearing with a husband who knew he had married a virgin. Taking another man's wife was therefore punishable by death in the Torah (Leviticus 20:10). Relations with a married woman constituted the sin of adultery, while seducing a virgin could be punished more lightly (Leviticus 22:16-17), sometimes only by a fine.

Unmarried women who were no longer virgins had an unsettled, uncontrolled status that was problematic for both their families and themselves.

Men and women with Israelite mothers but whose paternity was uncertain presented a particular challenge when it came to marriage since they could not marry most other Israelites. Mary Magdalene, like Jesus, might have been a mamzer, an Israelite whose paternity was doubtful and who was therefore restricted in terms of marriage prospects.

Modern scholarship refutes the medieval tradition of portraying Mary as a prostitute at the time she met Jesus. However, encouraging one's daughter to become a prostitute was prohibited, even if she was a financial burden. The punishment for promoting or allowing prostitution is not specified (Leviticus 19:29), and prostitution did exist in and around Israel. But the practice was blamed for harming the land. The rules of purity were based on the idea that Israel had been entrusted with a land to manage carefully so that it would remain fruitful. Sinful behavior created impurity and pushed Israel toward destruction. If Israelites ceased to follow the laws of purity, God threatened that the land itself would vomit them out (Leviticus 18:3-30).

Did Mary turn to prostitution before she met Jesus? Was she raped or exploited on her journey from Magdala? These are valid questions, but no text or reasonable inference from a text answers them. To confirm or deny these possibilities takes us beyond the available evidence. However, we can say that in Mary Magdalene's time and place, as in ours, individuals who were likely victims of sin were frequently depicted as sinners themselves.

Luke's reference to Mary's seven demons contributed to the Western tradition of portraying her as a prostitute. Common paintings depict her in extravagant attire, posing in front of a mirror, or abased in shame at Jesus' feet. Medieval piety associated vanity with prostitution, arguing that women sold themselves.

But regardless of the specifics of Mary Magdalene's past, what is clear is that in her time and place, women without the protection of a male family member were vulnerable to exploitation and abuse.

Marriage was seen as the best protection for a woman, and unmarried women past a certain age were seen as troublesome and liminal figures. The rules of purity and sexual conduct were designed to protect Israel's bloodlines and ensure the continuation of a fruitful land.

Despite the lack of concrete information about Mary Magdalene's past, she has become a powerful symbol for many people. For some, she represents the possibility of redemption and transformation, as she was said to have been exorcised of seven demons by Jesus. For others, she is a feminist icon, a woman who defied the gender norms of her time by following and supporting Jesus, even after his male disciples had abandoned him.

In recent years, there has been renewed interest in Mary Magdalene and her place in the early Christian movement. Some scholars have argued that she played a more significant role in Jesus' ministry than has traditionally been recognized and that her portrayal as a reformed prostitute may have been a way for later writers to diminish her importance. Others have focused on the ways in which Mary Magdalene's story has been shaped and reshaped by different cultural and historical contexts, and how her image continues to resonate with people today.

Mary Magdalene became popular as the patron saint of flagellants by the fourteenth century, and devotion to her and to the practice of self-inflicted pain was widespread. In one story of her life, she clawed at her skin until she bled, scored her breasts with stones, and tore out her hair, all as acts of penance for her self-indulgence. She long remained the ideal icon of mortification among the lay and clerical groups that encouraged similar penances. In 1375, an Italian fraternity of flagellants carried a banner during their processions as they whipped themselves; it depicts a giant enthroned Mary Magdalene. Her head reaches into the heavens and angels surround her. At her feet kneel four white hooded figures, whose robes leave a gap at the back for ritual scourging.

Where did people in the medieval world find the material to produce such an image? Certainly not from the New Testament or from early traditions concerning Mary Magdalene. The woman whom the flagellants venerated was a combination of two different Mary: Mary Magdalene and Mary of Egypt. Mary of Egypt is herself a classic figure of Christian folklore, the whore turned ascetic. In stories that began to circulate during the sixth century, Mary of Egypt, for the sake of Christ, gave up her practice of prostitution during a pilgrimage to Jerusalem in the fourth century and lived in a cave for the rest of her life. This story was spliced into Mary Magdalene's biography.

According to this expanded tale, most famous in the thirteenth-century form in which it appears in The Golden Legend of Jacobus de Voragine, Mary traveled to France fourteen years after the Resurrection, founding churches and removing idols. In this lush legend, Mary Magdalene is confused with a completely different person in the Gospels, Mary of Bethany. This confusion provides her with a sister she never had (Martha of Bethany) as well as with a brother she never had (Lazarus). She could count on help in her missionary work from her brother Lazarus and her sister Martha, along with the aid of a boatload of Christians who had come with her and her siblings to Marseilles. Then she retreated for thirty anorexic years to an isolated cave in Provence, where she was fed miraculously during her times of prayer and meditation, when angels lifted her up to heaven.

The deep ambivalence about sexuality held by those within monastic culture did not, however, quite allow them to give up thinking about how desirable this former prostitute must have been after her conversion. She is often depicted as nude in the craggy rocks of La Sainte-Baume. Her long and lustrous hair, covering the parts of her body that modesty conventionally requires to be covered, is a staple of iconography in the West to this day, making Mary Magdalene the Lady Godiva of Christian spirituality. Mary Magdalene approached the right rabbi when she sought out Jesus.

He reveled in his reputation for consorting with allegedly loose women (the word loose being applicable to any woman who did not bear her husband's or her father's name, or some other token of male protection). There were many unattached women among Jesus' disciples; when people called him "the friend of customs-agents and sinners" (Matthew 11:19), mat wasnot a compliment, and Jesus' critics ranked these female disciples among the "sinners."

Rabbi Jesus didn't mind damning his opponents in his defense of his female followers: "Amen I say to you, that customs-agents and whores precede you into the kingdom of God!" (Matthew 21:31). That is obviously not a general endorsement of tax collection and prostitution as methods of salvation, but a tough rejoinder to people who despised his followers and called his female disciples "whores." Mary Magdalene's persistent reputation for promiscuity in medieval legend and in many modern novels rests on the mistake of presuming that women with demons were necessarily promiscuous.

Exorcism in the ancient world was not only about sex, although scholars sometimes assume that describing a person as possessed denigrates that person, even after the cure. This was not the case: Ancient thinkers knew how to distinguish a person from his or her afflictions in a way their modern counterparts might learn from. When Mary first met him, Jesus had moved from Nazareth to Capernaum after a near stoning (Luke 4:16-30) convinced him that the parochial hamlet he had known from his childhood would never accept him as a rabbi. In Capernaum, he hit his stride. This fishing town of a couple thousand people provided him with a secure haven, and his reputation as an exorcist grew.

Jesus settled in with two brothers named Simon and Andrew, who had originally come from Bethsaida (John 1:44) and had married into a fishing family in Capernaum. Following a custom in Galilee, they moved in with their in-laws, so Simon's mother-in-law was an important member of a large extended family (Mark 1:29-31).

The sturdy basalt houses of Capernaum were small and packed with people. Most were one-story dwellings, although there were occasional two-story houses, as well. Few had courtyards, and since some people kept livestock, animals joined them from time to time in their cramped homes.

Accommodating Rabbi Jesus was not a routine act of hospitality. His own needs were modest enough for a prosperous family to support, although he admitted (Luke 7:34; Matthew 11:19) that he did have a reputation of eating and drinking a great deal. The strain came more from the eager crowds that thronged around him. Venues, where Jesus practiced exorcism and healing, could become so crowded that people were unable to move. The Gospels describe a scene in a house that was so crowded that four men had to break a hole through the roof and lower their paralyzed friend to Jesus on a litter to be healed (Matthew 9:1-8; Mark 2:1-12; Luke 5:17-26). That scene suggests the environment in which Mary Magdalene first met the young rabbi. Capernaum was abuzz with Jesus' reputation— you had to fight your way in to see him.

Time and again in the Gospels, people with unclean spirits and diseases are portrayed as taking the initiative and demanding Jesus' attention, often shouting out to him and pushing through crowds to touch him. Jesus exorcised and healed by the flow of Spirit that, he said, burst forth from him and tossed out demons for the sake of God's Kingdom (Matthew 12:28; Luke 11:20). These two forces—the Spirit and God's Kingdom— were central to his practice, and they were doubtless the two energies uppermost in his mind when he treated Mary Magdalene.

God's Kingdom was a new social order that, in the mind of Jesus and his followers, was already beginning to emerge and overthrow the rule of Rome and its dominance in the territory that it came to call Provincia Syria Palaestina. Rome's rule through its local underlings seemed to break every promise God had made to Israel. The chosen people were supposed to be secure in the Promised Land; the Gentiles, Isaiah had prophesied (Isaiah 25:6-12), would make pilgrimage to Mount Zion as supplicants, not victors.

In the midst of Jewish disappointment at the advent of Roman hegemony, Jesus announced this new, divine supremacy that the Aramaic Scriptures had promised: the malkhuta delahah, "the Kingdom of God." Jesus had memorized many of these texts (which differed in significant ways from Hebrew Scripture) when he was a child, embracing the complex, rich oral tradition that was the foundation of peasant life in first-century Syria Palaestina.

Like many other rabbis of his time, Jesus could not read or write. His learning came through oral traditions, and his peculiar genius found expression in his poetry of the divine Kingdom. He gave people like Mary the inner experience of God's power, which they felt was beginning to displace the demons, impurity, poverty, and brutish Roman rule that plagued their land. Jesus taught that God's Kingdom was the revolutionary principle behind the whole cosmos: One day all of life would shimmer with divine fullness and energy. Caesar's might would dissolve, and the Kingdom would push past any resistance with a force as natural and mysterious as a sprouting seed, as inexorable as rivers in flood. People loved to hear Jesus' vision of a new age, a complete transformation of the world as they knew it. They felt themselves transformed by the many parables he wove to take them into the world where divine justice and mercy would reign supreme and transform all humanity. In his exorcisms and healings, Jesus put this vision of the transformative Kingdom into action.

The Magdalene

The name of Mary Magdalene has been associated with sensuality, penitence, and devotion for almost 2,000 years, echoing in the churches and cloisters of Vezelay in Burgundy and Saint-Maximin in Provence. Thousands of pilgrims and tourists visit Vezelay's hilltop to see the simple, welcoming, and austere Romanesque Basilica that houses the Magdalene's supposed earthly remains. The remains, a bit of bone in a glass cylinder, are framed by metallic angels and cherubim in a darkened underground chapel. During my research for this book, I also visited Vezelay, where the Romanesque crypt attracts both curious tourists and devoted worshipers.

Although a little written notice beside Mary's relics complains about the Reformation and the French Revolution disrupting her remains, it adds nothing new to her story. That complaint is a common theme of antimodernist devotion to the Magdalene in France.

Claims about the Magdalene's darker history have circulated since the thirteenth century, suggesting that she was Jesus' wife or concubine. On July 22, 1209, Crusaders dispatched by the Pope burned the town of Beziers in response to the heretical teaching that Mary and Jesus had had sexual relations. Some fifteen thousand people died that day, including the heretics and those who protected them. Recent books have linked the legend that Jesus and Mary were lovers with the myth of the Holy Grail, suggesting that the Grail was Mary's womb—the holy vessel that gave birth to Jesus' children.

The Gospels name several female followers of Jesus, who became his disciples and gathered around him in Capernaum between 24 and 27 C.E. Despite their place in Jesus' movement being beyond doubt, many churches have ignored these women, claiming that Jesus chose only twelve male disciples. However, this confusion is due, in part, to the common tendency to confuse disciples with apostles and to attribute a stature to apostles that doesn't really reflect their role in Jesus' movement.

Therefore, Mary should not be denied her standing within nascent Christianity simply because she wasn't one of the Twelve.

The fact that Mary bore the nickname "Magdalene" among Jesus' followers supports the impression that she became part of his inner circle in Capernaum. Jesus gave such names to his closest disciples, after he had known them for an extended period. But we should not assume that the nickname was a compliment, as that was not Jesus' style.

During the Renaissance, portraits of Mary Magdalene often depicted her as a stylish urban lady before her encounter with Jesus, with jewelry, a low-cut dress, and beautifully coiffed hair. Instead of portraying her as a peasant fishmonger in a stained tunic, as she likely was, these depictions added to the later legends of Mary's wealth, elegance, and seductiveness. Church dogma considered that wealth often prompted self-indulgence and indolence, sins that were not in keeping with the humble and penitent Mary who is revered today.

EXORCISM

Luke's Gospel recounts that Jesus freed Mary from "seven demons" (8:2). This number inspired hagiographers in the Middle Ages to envision Mary as struggling with all seven Deadly Sins when she first encountered Jesus. According to The Golden Legend of Jacobus de Voragine, a compendium of stories of saints compiled in the thirteenth century, Mary was extremely wealthy and owned the towns of Magdala and Bethany near Jerusalem. However, her wealth, beauty, and youth led her down a path of temptation and degradation, ultimately leading her to become a common prostitute. Medieval teachers were fearful of this path for all women.

Beyond the mediaeval preoccupation with sin and sexuality, the number seven held symbolic meaning. Seven represented completeness in ancient Hebrew, Babylonian, and Persian numerology - the eternal rhythm of creation and rest in Genesis. Israel's fascination with the number represented a version of Babylonian wisdom based on astronomical observation. In ancient Near Eastern lunar calendars, the seven-day week represented the moon's phases: four quarters waxing and waning throughout the month. This calendar was adopted by Israel, and the seven-day week is written into the structure of nature itself in Genesis (1:3-2:3).

Because seven is the symbolic number of completion and fullness, mediaeval Catholicism conceived of seven Cardinal Virtues to balance the seven Deadly Sins. Hinduism's seven chakras represent the points where spiritual energy connects with our physical bodies. In this light, Mary's "seven" demons should be viewed. The ancient mind's inherent symbolism of seven was so strong that the reference to seven demons in Luke's text does not have to be taken literally.

Mary likely underwent multiple exorcisms, which probably took about a year. Through this process, she emerged as one of Jesus' key disciples. Unlike other exorcists of his time, Jesus openly acknowledged the difficulty and danger of dealing with unclean spirits.

We don't know how many times Jesus met with Mary, and the Gospels are silent about what occurred during these sessions. Elsewhere in the New Testament (as in many other ancient pieces of literature), narrators enjoyed recounting tales of demonic possession. The possessed often shrieked, shredded their clothing, and ripped their flesh - displays that storytellers found hard to resist. However, Mary Magdalene's exorcism did not involve this type of public drama; Jesus appeared to have treated her privately.

During this lengthy healing, Jesus initiated Mary into his unique understanding of exorcism. Exorcism provides insight into Rabbi Jesus' understanding of the role of the divine Spirit in the world. He referred to demons as "unclean spirits," a term later adopted by Christian writers. People were as pure in Jesus' eyes as God created Adam and Eve. It was not solely due to contact with external objects that a person became impure or unclean. Impurity, on the other hand, was a disturbance in that person's own spirit - the "unclean spirit" - which caused them to want to be impure. Uncleanness, according to Jesus, stemmed from a disturbed desire that people had to pollute and harm themselves.

Uncleanness needed to be dealt with in the inward, spiritual personality of those afflicted. "There is nothing outside the person proceeding into one that can defile one, but what proceeds out of the person is what defiles the person" (Mark 7:15). That is why contact with people considered sinners and impure did not bother Jesus, an attitude that scandalized conventional Pharisaic teachers.

Jesus believed that God's Spirit was a more powerful force than the unclean spirits that troubled humanity. Against demonic infection, a greater force or counter contagion could prevail - the positive energy of God's purity. Defilement was an interior force of uncleanness that needed to be identified and banished by the energy of Spirit.

When Jesus taught his disciples about exorcism, he recognized the issue of serial possession, which Mary had experienced.

This teaching appears in Luke's Gospel shortly after the mention of Mary's possession (11:24-26; see also Matthew 12:43-45): "When an unclean spirit leaves a person, it travels through waterless places in search of rest, and when it finds none, it declares, 'I will return to my house from whence I came.'" It travels and discovers it swept and adorned. Then it proceeds, bringing with it seven other spirits eviler than itself, and entering dwells there. And that person's endings are worse than their beginnings."

Rabbi Jesus the exorcist speaks in this passage based on a practitioner's familiarity with demonic behavior. He knows that an unclean spirit, once out of a person, will try to find somewhere to go ("seeking repose"), and perhaps will decide to return to the person it came from ("my house"). An exorcist was not successful if a person was left in a clean-furnished house with open doors and windows waiting for a squatter. That just invited demonic repossession.

Jesus pulls back from any sweeping claim of instantly effective exorcistic power and disparages the results of quick-fix exorcisms. In contrast, the Gospels sporadically make general statements to the effect that Jesus effortlessly exorcised demons. His own words belie that claim. His reference to the demon joining up with "other spirits eviler than itself—seven!" echoes the description of Mary's possession. We cannot conclude that Jesus had Mary in mind here; after all, she was possessed by a total of seven demons in Luke's description, while Jesus spoke of seven additional demons. But her case exemplified his concern: a possession that an incautious exorcist might make repeatedly worse.

To break the cycle of possession, Jesus taught that divine Spirit had to be installed where demons had been. Mary must have been aware of how desperate she had once been, as well as the triumph her cure entailed. She required intelligence, insight, and sympathy to see Jesus' lengthy treatment through to completion. According to Rabbi Jesus' teaching, the Magdalene felt herself healed by an inner seismic shift with literally cosmic consequences because it signaled the world's transformation by the arrival of God's Kingdom.

Jesus was not always a gentle therapist. He and his followers insisted on ultimate combat with every demon because each unclean spirit represented them all. Mary became the living, breathing embodiment of the ascendance and power of Spirit. And for all the twists and turns of Christian legend, she has always stood for personal victory over evil.

Mary appears to be a mirror image of Jesus in her stark depiction of the evil she had overcome. According to the Golden Legend, Christ "embraced her in all his life," emphasizing that she became his intimate friend, constant companion, and source of help on his journeys. Petrarch referred to her as "God's sweet friend" ("dulcis arnica dei"). Here, legend develops in a way that helps us see more clearly what is already implicit in the most ancient sources: a close and lasting bond between Jesus and Mary.

But Jesus rejected these accusations and instead claimed that his power came from the Holy Spirit, which was a far greater force than any unclean spirit. He taught his disciples that exorcism was not just a matter of casting out demons, but also of replacing the void left by their departure with the positive energy of God's purity.

Jesus specifically acknowledges the problem of serial possession, which Mary had experienced, in Luke's Gospel. He teaches that once an unclean spirit has been cast out of a person, it will seek to return and may even bring other spirits with it, worsening the person's situation. To prevent repeated possession, Jesus emphasizes the importance of installing divine Spirit where demons had been.

Mary's healing involved a seismic shift in her inner being, which signaled the arrival of God's Kingdom according to Rabbi Jesus' teaching. Although Jesus was not always gentle in his approach to exorcism, he and his followers insisted on ultimate combat with each and every demon because each unclean spirit represented them all. Mary became the embodiment of the power of Spirit and an example of personal victory over evil.

Legend has developed around Mary and her relationship with Jesus, emphasizing their close and lasting bond. Jesus' opponents accused him of being in league with the powers of darkness because of his intimate relationship with Mary and his ability to cast out demons. But Jesus rejected these accusations and continued to teach his disciples about the importance of replacing the void left by the departure of unclean spirits with the positive energy of God's purity.

In its origin, the name Beelzebub has roots in the ancient pagan traditions of the Middle East. Beelzebul, the god of the underworld, was called upon in spells and sorcery during the time of Jesus to drive away demons of disease. Thus, in the context of exorcism in first-century Galilee, Jesus' Jewish opponents' accusations against him amounted to a charge of black magic.

In response, Rabbi Jesus reacted with his trademark rage and disregard for logic. He maintained that his exorcisms, like those of the Pharisees who opposed him, were beneficial. He emphasized that his exorcisms were unique in that they signaled the approaching of God's Kingdom, which would overthrow Satan's dominion. (Matthew 12:24–28)

The Pharisees accused Jesus of not being able to cast out demons except by the power of Beelzebul, ruler of the demons. Jesus retorted by questioning the logic of Satan casting out Satan, arguing that any kingdom divided against itself would be wasted. He then challenged the Pharisees by asking, "And if I by Beelzebul cast out demons, by whom do your sons cast them out?" He concluded by saying that if he cast out demons by God's Spirit, then the kingdom of God had arrived.

For Jesus and his followers, sensitivity to the world of the spirits, clean and unclean, did not disqualify Mary Magdalene as a disciple, any more than her rabbi's reputation for tackling demons with Beelzebul's authorization disqualified him as an exorcist. In fact, Jesus taught that engaging impure spirits, for all the danger involved, was what dislodged Satan from preeminence in the world, as God's Spirit ushered in God's Kingdom.

In Jesus' teachings, contact with the divine transformed unclean spirits with God's Spirit and removed their impure influence. Mary became a living symbol in Jesus' movement of the Spirit by which Jesus removed unclean spirits and brought the divine Kingdom into the human world.

A commentator in the twelfth century noted that Mary's companionship with Jesus would not have been permitted in the Church of his day. He explained that women were allowed "among the Jews" to "go about with religious men," demonstrating that he understood Judaism better than some modern interpreters. Although historical scholarship has progressed in many ways since the Middle Ages, there has been a regression in the understanding of women's and feminine roles within Judaism. Despite evidence to the contrary, modern Christians continue to propagate the false claim that women had no place in Jewish worship and learning leadership.

Mary's gender presented no obstacle to her growing influence among Jesus' disciples. In fact, being a woman was consonant with her emerging power and authority as an expert on exorcism. Rabbi Jesus conceived of the divine Spirit, the force that dissolved unclean spirits, as feminine.

Since the time of the book of Proverbs (that is, the sixth century B.C.E.), Spirit has had a secure place in Israelite theology as Yahweh's female partner. The force of Spirit that rushed out from God at the beginning of the cosmos and filled the entire universe was feminine both in the noun's gender (ruach in Hebrew) and in the life-giving creativity with which Spirit endowed creation. This divine feminine was closely associated with Wisdom, the eternal consort of Yahweh (Proverbs 8:22-31):

Yahweh possessed me at the beginning of his way, Before his works of old. From everlasting I was established, From the beginning, before the earth... When he established the heavens, I was there, When he drew a circle on the face of the deep.

When he made firm the skies above, When the fountains of the deep grew strong, When he placed the boundary of the sea, And waters did not transgress his command, When he marked the foundations of the earth, I was beside him as an architect, and I was daily his delight, Rejoicing before him always, Rejoicing in his inhabited world, And my delight was with the sons of men.

The intimacy between Wisdom and Yahweh was so deep and enjoyable that it could be described in erotic terms, and the human delight in Wisdom also promised a life of deep, rewarding pleasure. Just as God might appear by means of the three men who visited Abraham and Sarah at Mamre (Genesis 18:1-15), so divine Spirit conveyed herself with feminine traits. God's majesty was inconceivably great and varied, and it incorporated feminine as well as masculine identity.

Jesus said he spoke on behalf of Wisdom (Sophia in the Greek text of Luke) and counted himself among her envoys to the world (Luke 11:49): "Therefore also the Wisdom of God said, 'I will send them prophets and apostles, some of whom they will kill and persecute.'" Just as Jesus sent his delegates into Galilee, so he believed Wisdom had delegated him to repair a broken world. In Rabbi Jesus' mind, his whole movement amounted to an apostolic message from Spirit and therefore from Wisdom.

Western Christianity's fixation since the Middle Ages on an exclusively masculine deity tragically departs from Jesus' conception of God. Even the term for Spirit, which is feminine in Hebrew, becomes neuter in Greek and masculine in Latin, as if the process of translation itself conspired against his thought. Yet at the wellspring of his movement, male and female together reflected the reality of the divine image (Genesis 1:27), and God's Spirit conveyed the full feminine force of divinity.

We have observed that Jesus performed an exorcism on Mary Magdalene over the course of about a year, and during this time, she became more knowledgeable about his exorcism techniques than anyone else.

As a result, she became one of his primary disciples and an expert in dealing with demonic forces. Mary embodied Jesus' audacious claim in Matthew 12:28, "If I cast out demons by the power of God's Spirit, then the kingdom of God has come upon you!" This gave her a special place among his disciples because she represented the arrival of God's Kingdom. However, neither the Gospels nor scholarship recognize Mary's role as a teacher who related Jesus' exorcisms and their significance.

In other cases in the Gospels, scholars identify a source within the Gospels attributed to a prominent disciple, such as Peter, who had a similar close connection to Jesus in relation to stories or teachings. For example, Peter was the primary source of the Transfiguration story, in which he and two other apostles witnessed Jesus transformed with heavenly light and speaking with Moses and Elijah (Mark 9:2-8). Peter was the teacher within Jesus' movement who passed on this story and shaped its meaning until it was written down in the Gospels.

The Gospels do not identify their authors by name. Instead, each is simply called "According to Mark," "According to Matthew," "According to Luke," and "According to John," without any indication of who these authors were. Scholars must infer how the Gospels were produced, by whom, and in what communities of early Christians from the texts themselves.

Despite the uncertainties involved, from the start of the second century onward, thoughtful readers have recognized that the Gospels are not simply books written by individual authors working alone. Rather, they are composite editions of differing sources put together by different communities in the generations after Jesus' death. It is therefore vital to identify and analyze the Gospel sources to get at the best evidence about Jesus and to understand how the Gospels developed as literature.

One of these crucial sources was provided by Peter and his followers. They prepared people for baptism by reciting an oral narrative of what God had accomplished through Jesus.

In the Greco-Roman world, this was a complex and potentially dangerous process, as opposed to the routine baptism of infants in modern practice. During the first century, Jesus' worship was tolerated at best, and violent local pogroms occasionally erupted against the strange new Christian "superstition" (as the Romans categorized Jesus' movement). Because Christianity was perceived as a strange form of Judaism, Christians could be drawn into violent outbursts against Jews. As a result, someone claiming to want to be baptized in Jesus' name could be an informant for a city magistrate or, worse, a gang of narrow-minded thugs.

A typical year of probation was customary for converts, not only to assess their sincerity but also to ensure that they had fully learned the congregation's patterns of behavior, rituals, and prayers, refused idolatry, trusted wholeheartedly in the one God, and dedicated themselves to a life of the Spirit while resisting the material world. All these elements were integral to the Christian message, which each Gospel conveyed to its community based on earlier oral evangelism.

Peter was particularly involved in preparing converts for baptism, and passages in the Gospels that explicitly mention him or relate to his baptismal agenda likely originated from him. When scholars associate a disciple's name with their ritual agenda and the oral source they developed, they establish a kind of signature within the source. Peter is repeatedly named in passages crucial to preparing converts for baptism, indicating that he had a profound impact on shaping the Gospels.

Applying the same logic and evidence to Mary Magdalene, she emerges as the author of a source of stories that bear her oral signature. She was the most significant source of stories about Jesus' exorcisms. Because of her experience and standing, simply following Jesus put her in an ideal position to craft the detailed exorcism stories we read in the Gospels. These stories, read in order (Mark 1:21-28, 5:1-17, 9:14-29), provide a manual for dealing with unclean spirits by identifying them, confronting them with divine Spirit, and proclaiming their defeat.

They also reflect a progressive development in Jesus' ability to cope with increasingly difficult cases of possession.

The first story in the Magdalene source comes from early in Jesus' time in Capernaum, around 24 C.E. (Mark 1:21-28). The second reflects the period beginning with his flight from Herod Antipas in 27 C.E. (Mark 5:1-17), and the third appears after Jesus' Transfiguration in 30 C.E. (Mark 9:14-29). Recognizing these three exorcism stories as the core of Mary's source allows other stories to fit naturally as tributaries.

The first exorcism story, set in the Capernaum synagogue, depicts unclean spirits whose threat dissolves once they are confronted with purity (Mark 1:21-28). A close reading of the account reveals Mary Magdalene's oral signature, reflecting her insider's knowledge of the deep inner struggle involved in exorcism for a person who was possessed.

Capernaum was prosperous enough to have an actual structure for its synagogue, where the Jewish population could gather to settle local disputes, hear and discuss Scripture, delegate priestly duties, collect and transfer taxes to the Temple, and participate in rituals such as circumcision and burial. This first public act of Jesus in the Gospel According to Mark unfolds in a dignified space, a small building equipped with benches.

Mary's story describes a situation where Jesus' routine is interrupted by an unclean spirit in the synagogue. While the demon "speaks," the people in the synagogue can only hear inarticulate shrieks. However, Jesus alone understands the meaning of the sounds. The demon identifies itself with all unclean demons of the spirit world in a fascinating switch of pronouns in the text (here italicized; Mark 1:24): "*We* have nothing for you, Nazarene Jesus! Have you come to destroy *us*? I know who you are—the holy one of God!"

The slip back and forth between plural and singular has surprised many readers of Mark's text. Multiple demons—like the seven in Mary's story and the demon who found seven colleagues to repossess a person in Jesus' saying (Luke 11:24-26; Matthew 12:43-45)—signaled the resistance of the demonic world as a whole. Jesus viewed the violence of demons as part of the impending defeat of their regime, like a military commander who claims that acts by insurgents only prove they are desperate. In addition to its identification with unclean spirits as a whole, the demon in the synagogue also specifies the purpose of Jesus' exorcisms: not simple banishment, but their definitive removal from power. That is what the demon fears on behalf of the whole realm of unclean spirits: regime change instigated by Jesus as the agent of God's Kingdom, the kind of demonic retreat Mary Magdalene had experienced.

Fearing destruction, the unclean spirits act before Jesus speaks, initiating a preemptive strike by naming him. The word exorcise (ex-orkjzo in Mark's Greek) means to adjure or "to bind with an oath" (which is the aim of an exorcism). The oath was a formula that exorcists usually used to invoke divine power and force demons to obey their commands. Such spells were more effective when they identified a demon by name. In this case, however, the demon jumps in with a spell and a naming of its own. In effect, it is exorcising the exorcist, a notable departure from the well-documented form of exorcism stories in the ancient world.

Mary's source describes this as a very noisy event. The demon "cried out" (Mark 1:23). Jesus shouted back in the rough language of the street, "Shut up, and get out from him!" (v. 25). The demon's obedience came under protest; it "convulsed" its nameless victim and departed with a scream (v. 26). These acute observations all point toward a storyteller with keen knowledge of the deep combat with evil that Jesus' exorcisms involved, their raucous quality, and the danger that the exorcist would be defeated. Moreover, the storyteller knew how Jesus interpreted the demons' wordless shout (Mark 1:34), as an admission of ultimate defeat. Whoever conveyed this story had to have known both what went on and what Jesus thought about it. Mary Magdalene best fits the description of that storyteller.

By taking Mary's influence into account, we can understand why, unlike most ancient stories of exorcism, Mark's narratives depict the demons' violent resistance to Jesus instead of portraying him as a self-confident exorcist. This comes out most vividly in the second story from the Magdalene source, which is set in Decapolis, just on the other side of the Sea of Galilee from Magdala.

Several striking images, such as the possessed man's residence in a cemetery, his habit of self-harm, and his location in Gentile territory, suggest that this exorcism was aimed at addressing uncleanness as the evil that Jesus targeted in all of his exorcisms. The possessed man embodies everything unholy and is named "legion" to emphasize the source of the contagion. When Rabbi Jesus exorcised demons, he acted on behalf of the possessed, but he also acted against the source of impurity, which was Rome and Rome's collaborator, Herod Antipas.

Mary Magdalene, whose town was adjacent to Antipas's new capital, understood the reality of this uncleanness. The narrative emphasizes the struggle involved in this exorcism, as the demons were numerous, talked back to Jesus, and did not obey a direct command. The legion story deliberately engages in exaggeration, making it challenging for commentators to distinguish the story's symbolic meaning from the literal event it depicts. Nevertheless, the symbolic meaning remains clear no matter how literally we take the details: as the divine Kingdom takes root, Rome will be dislodged. Removing impurity by naming it made Satan fall, as other teachings of Jesus confirm.

Jesus became increasingly prophetic, and his words and deeds took on the character of signs, indicating how God was acting or about to act in the world. Mary Magdalene told the story of the legion of demons from the sympathetic perspective of someone who could speak from firsthand experience of being exorcised. She knew the real depth of the cosmic antagonism involved in Jesus' exorcism and had felt that antagonism in her own body.

The exorcism stories from Mary's source reflect Jesus' method of magnifying awareness that all impurity dissolves in the holiness of Spirit. In the first story, set in Capernaum's synagogue, the demon defeated itself by acknowledging the purity it confronted in Jesus, "the holy one of God," and Jesus' technique could involve giving unclean spirits what they said they wanted to speed their departure.

In the third significant story, which involves a severely possessed child, Jesus assures the anguished father that "anything is possible to one who believes" (Mark 9:23). Faith sets the stage for successful therapy, and Mary's devoted discipleship, exemplified by her journey with Jesus from Capernaum to Jerusalem, symbolizes the atmosphere of effective treatment.

Scholars have yet to scrutinize Mary's impact on the Gospels with the same intensity that they have examined Peter's, Paul's, James's, or Barnabas's. While they have had access to the relevant information in the Gospels and refined their analytic tools regarding other disciples and their sources, they have disregarded or minimized Mary's explicit connection to Jesus' exorcisms and overlooked evidence suggesting that Mary was the one who shaped and conveyed the stories of Jesus' exorcisms in the Gospels. For almost two millennia, Mary Magdalene's voice has echoed anonymously in the Gospels. It is now time to identify the speaker and appreciate her words.

Listening to Mary Magdalene's account can help us understand not only Mary herself but also a profoundly charismatic and prophetic aspect of Christianity that firmly opposes the forces of uncleanness with the power of God's Spirit.

Not all of Jesus' followers always embraced the violence of his exorcisms. We learn of this not from the Magdalene source but from other material that explains Jesus' exorcistic theory in his own words and depicts his conflict with those around him. This teaching confirms, from Jesus' perspective, precisely the sense of cosmic struggle and resistance that the Magdalene source narrates.

According to Mark's Gospel, Jesus' family once attempted to physically restrain him, perceiving him as "out of his mind" (3:21). To those who did not share Jesus' vision, he could easily appear to be mentally unstable. Rabbis during this period also described another mystic, Simon ben Zoma, as "out of his mind" because he experienced ecstasy amid everyday life.

His family's well-intentioned, conventional worry for Jesus only fueled his determination to confront Satan (Mark 3:22—27). He insisted that he was not crazy or possessed by Beelzebul. Instead, he directly battled "the strong man," the leader of all demons, in his exorcisms. Jesus stated, "No one can enter the strong man's house to plunder his goods unless he first binds the strong man; then he can plunder his house" (v. 27). Once he bound the strong man, Jesus could seize his possessions!

Jesus did not want to leave a possessed person's body open for unclean spirits to return to with even more impure companions. Instead, he would evict Satan from the house. He believed that Satan's defeat signaled the arrival of the Kingdom, and the Spirit of God, whom Jesus conceived of as female in his theology, accomplished both. When the Spirit moves in this world, she displaces demons and establishes divine justice. That is why, when discussing his exorcisms, Jesus said that denying the Holy Spirit was the only unforgivable sin (Mark 3:28-30): "Truly I tell you, people will be forgiven for their sins and whatever blasphemies they utter; but whoever blasphemes against the Holy Spirit can never have forgiveness, but is guilty of an eternal sin." The unpardonable sin is to reject the Holy Spirit as she transforms the world by vanquishing evil. The consistency of Jesus' thinking on exorcism is notable and echoes the Magdalene source.

Luke's naming of Mary in personal connection with repeated exorcisms allows us to infer that Mary Magdalene told stories about Jesus, particularly about his exorcisms, which are recounted in the Gospels today. She stands alongside the apostles who influenced how Jesus' message was preached and taught, and the exorcism stories in the Gospels bear her signature.

One of Jesus' most enduring teachings that she helped shape was about how the power from God could dissolve evil by allowing it to name itself for what it was, and she demonstrated how he put that teaching into practice. Medieval legend conveyed Mary's importance in this field in its own way. For instance, Gherardesca da Pisa, who died in 1269, described Mary as intervening in her own bloody battle with a demon and then helping her tend to her wounds.

Mary understood that the demons' most fearsome weapon, which they deployed to resist Jesus' exorcisms, was their unique knowledge of his identity. Until the first exorcism story in Mark, no one in the Gospel had referred to Jesus as "the holy one of God," a phrase that no one else would use again. By telling stories like this, Mary indicated that she knew this secret. The nameless man in the synagogue in Capernaum alone identified Jesus as "the holy one of God," while the man with the legion of demons uniquely called Jesus "Son of highest God" (Mark 5:7). As Jesus' companion in exorcism, Mary Magdalene understood that his struggle with the demons involved this messianic secret.

These inarticulate demonic cries raise a question: If the demons alone knew Jesus' spiritual identity, and he alone understood what they said, to whom did he disclose this knowledge? Once again, Mary Magdalene's oral signature leads the way to an answer. The first exorcism in Mark distinguishes Jesus as "the holy one of God," and then explains what that phrase means. The demon is an "unclean spirit," as it is elsewhere in the Gospels. As we have seen, impurity, according to Jesus' analysis, resides within a human being rather than in external objects. That which defiles originates within and spreads outward, rather than the other way around. This idea is crucial to the plot. Possession, according to Rabbi Jesus, occurred only with a person's tacit consent or inadvertence, allowing impurity to be removed through conscious intention.

The synagogue's unclean spirit, a source of impurity, identified Jesus as a source of purity, "the holy one of God." That is why the presence of Jesus posed a threat to that demon and the demonic world as a whole. The unspecified number of demons in the synagogue, the "legion" in the cemetery, the demon who resisted Jesus' disciples, and the "seven" who left Mary Magdalene all point to the demonic axis as a whole. Because the unclean spirits recognized purity when they experienced it, the spiritual conflict between Jesus and the forces of impurity was resolved.

Violent though their rebellion seemed, the demons ultimately recognized their own nonexistence. Their only power was denial. They could rebel against God's pure purpose, but only with the empty complaint of their own impotence. Finally, the demons had no power at all. They drowned in their own knowledge as surely as the legion did once they revealed themselves in the pigs. According to Mary's account, Rome was also headed toward the same fate.

The perspective through which the Gospels detail stories of exorcism reveals that Mary Magdalene drew from her own experiences. She had personally known the violent conflict within her own body between the demons and Jesus' desire to permanently expel them from her. The opening demonic scream, "We have nothing for you," is mirrored in the story of the man with a legion of demons. The tormented man cries out, "I have nothing for you" (Mark 5:7), and it becomes evident that "I" conceals a demonic multitude. Mary had experienced contrary and convulsive forces within her body and mind that once caused her to be at odds with herself, leading her to be controlled by impulses not her own. However, when faced with the knowledge of purity, what once seemed threatening in impurity dissolved. Obsessions ceased, and conscious choice replaced being driven by desires that were not her own. Purity within meant bodily integrity and cleanliness in action, which is the wisdom behind Jesus' exorcisms. This was wisdom that Mary had gained from her own experiences, and it made her proud to bear the nickname "the Magdalene."

Mary's role in the development of the Gospels has often been overlooked. However, it is time to acknowledge that she was a principal source in understanding Jesus' legacy. Mary's influence on how the founders of Christianity perceived the Spirit moving in the world would have been of great interest to Marguerite. The Magdalene's crucial contribution to how people in the first century understood Jesus' teachings about confronting evil in this world with the Spirit that ushers in the Kingdom of God would have assured Marguerite that someone was indeed there for her both beyond heaven's gate and in the daily struggles of life.

Jesus Teachings in the Gospel of Mary

The teachings of the Savior are at the heart of the Gospel of Mary, and Jesus is the central figure in salvation. His teachings are the key to eternal life with God, and he is referred to as the Lord and Savior. The interpretation of his teachings in the Gospel of Mary, on the other hand, differs significantly from other common understandings. While it acknowledges Jesus' death and resurrection, these events are not central to Christian belief, but rather the occasion for the disciples' mission to preach the gospel. Instead, the Gospel of Mary focuses on Jesus as a teacher and intermediary of divine revelation.

According to the Savior, after death, the human body disintegrates into the elements from which it was formed, and only the spiritual soul is immortal and lives forever. This knowledge leads people to the realization that they are spiritual beings created in the image of God, and it enables them to overcome the worldly attachments and bodily passions that lead to suffering and death. As a result, the ultimate goal of salvation is not the resurrection of the body at the end of the age, but the ascension of the soul to God, both in this life through following the Savior's teachings and at the death when the bonds between the body and the soul are loosened beyond time and eternity.

The Gospel of Mary does not teach hell or eternal punishment because God is not portrayed as a wrathful ruler or judge, but rather as the Good. Gender, sexuality, and social roles are all seen as part of the lower material realm, so God is not called Father. Even human beings' true spiritual nature is non-gendered, and they are neither male nor female, but simply Human in accordance with the divine Image of the transcendent Good. The focus of moral effort is on inner spiritual transformation rather than sin and judgement. Service to others is primarily defined as teaching people to obey the Savior's words and preaching the gospel of the Divine Realm.

The establishment of excessive laws and rules within the Christian community is seen as a tool for domination and is unnecessary for proper order.

These teachings were shaped not only in conversation and controversy with other Christians but also, as we will see, in the crucibles of ancient intellectual and social life among the diverse societies under Roman imperial rule. While Jesus and most of his earliest followers were Jews, Christianity quickly spread around the edges of the Eastern Mediterranean, from Rome to Egypt, attracting Gentile followers as well as Jews living outside of Judaea/Palestine. The earliest existing Christian literature, the letters of Paul, documents the spread of Christianity through Asia Minor to the imperial capital of Rome itself during the first decades after the death of Jesus in Jerusalem. When Gentiles encountered the teachings of Jesus, many of the earlier connections to Jewish faith and practice receded, while the belief systems and world views of the new Gentile Christians brought other issues to the fore. Tensions over whether Gentiles who accepted Jesus needed to be circumcised or follow dietary laws gave way to other concerns. Some elements already in the Jesus tradition became more prominent, especially when they intersected with philosophical speculation and popular pieties. The Gospel of Mary provides one example of these kinds of Christianity.

The Gospel of Mary presents many familiar sayings of Jesus, but they are interpreted in a framework that may seem foreign to modern readers used to reading the literature of the New Testament as part two of the Bible, following the Hebrew Scriptures of the Old Testament. Interpreting Jesus' and his followers' lives and actions as fulfilments of Hebrew Scriptures was critical to early Christian claims that faith in Christ had surpassed Judaism and that Christians were the true Israel. By the fourth and fifth centuries, this viewpoint had earned the title of orthodoxy and had condemned other points of view as heretical.

The Gospel of Mary can be viewed as an interpretation of Jesus' teachings by someone familiar with ancient philosophical piety but lacking knowledge of Judaism. It's worth noting that the prevailing perspective of orthodoxy may be so powerful and pervasive that modern readers may find the teachings "strange," as Andrew did. However, early Christians drew heavily upon popular Greek and Roman philosophy and piety, which can be seen in the canonical literature of the New Testament. Despite being written in the second century, the Gospel of Mary reflects an interpretation stream that extends far back into the early decades of first-century Christianity. Therefore, it is important to consider this work as a valuable source of insight into early Christian thought and practice.

To fully comprehend how Jesus' teachings were received among those who adhered to Platonism and Stoicism, it is necessary to provide a brief overview of some of the ideas from those traditions that most strongly intersected with the Gospel of Mary's teachings. Plato, who lived centuries before the writing of the Gospel of Mary, argued that true wisdom comes from cultivating the soul, not indulging in physical pleasures. According to Plato, death is merely the release of the soul from the body, so the wise prioritize the eternal well-being of the soul over the immediate desires of the body. Only by disciplining the body and minimizing physical contact and associations can the soul truly grasp the truth of its own nature and the truth of Reality.

When the Gospel of Mary was written, ideas from Platonists and Stoics had become pervasive in popular culture in the eastern Mediterranean. Similarly, we modern Americans are all armchair psychologists, talking about childhood traumas, neuroses, and complexes, irrespective of having read Freud. The ideas of these ancient thinkers had become removed from their original literary and intellectual contexts, and had spread over a vast geographical area, encompassing diverse cultures under the Roman empire. As a result, the social, political, and intellectual contexts within which people reflected upon such topics as human nature, justice, and ethics had shifted. In the pluralistic mix of ancient urban life, ideas that had been separate and logically incompatible began to coexist.

For instance, the Stoic ideal of apatheia could be neatly grafted onto a Platonizing, dualistic conception of ethics as conflict between the body and the immaterial soul.

Historians have a good understanding of how elite philosophers in the early Roman Empire developed Platonic and Stoic ideas. However, less is known about how these ideas were conveyed to the general population and how they were interpreted and utilized by the vast semi-literate or illiterate majority. If the Gospel of Mary is any indication of popular thought, it is evident that the teachings of Plato had evolved in ways that would have certainly surprised him. The portrait of a resurrected Jesus instructing his followers to tend to their immortal souls and eliminate their passions in the Stoic tradition so that, upon death, they can outsmart and defeat the wicked Powers who will try to impede them on their heavenly journey indicates that we have come a long way from the intellectual discussions of the male elite in Athens. By comparing the Gospel of Mary's ideas with those of Plato and the Stoics, we can to some extent determine the differences between them. There are four key similarities: the association of evil with material nature, the necessity for accurate knowledge of Reality to liberate the soul from the influence of passions, an ethical focus on conforming to the pattern of the Good, and the ascent of the soul to the Divine Realm after death.

The Body and the Word

The relationship between the body and the world has been debated by philosophers for centuries. The Gospel of Mary, an ancient Christian text, provides a unique perspective on this relationship. It is a dialogue between the Savior and his disciples. The conversation begins with a question from a disciple about the nature of the material universe. The Savior replies by saying that all material things are interconnected, have no ultimate spiritual value, and will dissolve back into their original condition, which he calls their "root."

This question and answer reflect the influence of contemporary philosophical debates about whether matter is preexistent or created. If matter is preexistent, then it is eternal, and if it is created, then it is subject to destruction. The Savior agrees that matter has no form or qualities of its own; it is simply the underlying substance that is subject to being formed or produced. He believes that everything will dissolve back into its own proper root, whether it is the result of natural causes, whether it has been molded out of formlessness, or whether it has been created from nothing. His point is clear: because the material realm is entirely destined for dissolution, it is temporary, and therefore the world and the body have no ultimate spiritual value.

Both Plato and the Gospel of Mary propose that there are two natures, one belonging to the material world and one to the Divine Realm. Evil belongs only in the material world and is associated with the finite and changing character of material reality. The nature of the Divine Realm is perfect goodness, unchanging, and eternal. The material world is the place of suffering and death, while the Divine Realm offers immortality in peace. The dualism between the material and the Divine is sharper in the Gospel of Mary than in Plato, but the Savior does not argue that the material world is evil and will be destroyed. He argues that the material world is destined to dissolve back into its original root-nature.

The idea that the world is fleeting is not new to Christian thought. Paul wrote that "the form of this world is passing away," and the Gospel of Mark says that "heaven and earth will pass away." However, the difference between these traditional Christian views and the perspective presented in the Gospel of Mary is in the understanding of what happens after the dissolution of the material world. In the traditional Christian view, the dissolution of the material world is seen as the prelude to a new creation, a new world in which righteousness dwells, and believers will live eternally with God. But in the Gospel of Mary, there is no mention of a new creation. The dissolution of the material world is understood as the final state when everything that is now mixed up together will be separated and return to its proper "root" - the material to its formless nature or nothingness, and the spiritual to its root in the Good.

This understanding of the ultimate fate of the world raises the question of how one should live in the face of the fleeting nature of the material world. The book of 2 Peter addresses this question directly, stating that "what sort of person ought you to be in lives of holiness and godliness, waiting for and hastening the coming of the day of God, because of which the heavens will be kindled and dissolved, and the elements will melt with fire!" In other words, the understanding that the material world is temporary and ultimately destined for dissolution should inspire us to live a life of holiness and godliness, as we look forward to the day when all things will be made right.

The Gospel of Mary presents a sharper dualism between the material and the Divine realm than is found in Plato. According to the Gospel, the nature of evil belongs only in the material world, and the nature of the Divine is perfect goodness, unchanging, and eternal.

Sin, Judgement and law

According to the Gospel of Mary, sin is the mixing of spiritual and material natures. The material world cannot serve as the basis for determining good and evil because attachment to it leads to sinful human conditions. Instead, one should focus on the spiritual self to attain peace of heart.

The Gospel of Mary diverges from the traditional Christian doctrine of original sin, which holds that all humans are inherently sinful due to the actions of Adam and Eve in the Garden of Eden. Instead, the text presents a more Gnostic view where the human soul is fundamentally pure and good, but trapped in a material body that is prone to deception and passion.

For the Gospel of Mary, the sin of the world is a state of ignorance and separation from one's true spiritual nature rather than a moral or legal transgression. The Savior's message focuses primarily on guiding the soul towards enlightenment and union with God, rather than emphasizing the need for repentance and forgiveness of sins. The text also stresses that matter is ultimately transient and inferior to the spiritual realm, and that the ultimate goal of the human being is to transcend the material world and return to their true spiritual nature.

In short, the Gospel of Mary provides a unique perspective on sin and the nature of human beings compared to orthodox Christian theology. The text highlights the importance of spiritual enlightenment and transcendence over moral rules and regulations and asserts that the true self is not the material body but rather the soul infused with the spirit.

The Son of Man

The phrase "Son of Man" in the Gospel of Mary is believed to mean "rrcyHpe SnpcuMe" in Coptic. This phrase represents the child of true humanity and the image of the divine realm that resides within every person. It is considered the true representation of humanity's spiritual nature and the ideal to which the disciples should aspire.

The Savior tells the disciples that "The child of true humanity exists within you" and commands them to "follow it! Those who search for it will find it". Following the child of true humanity requires identifying with the archetypal image of humanity and conforming to it as a model. This is in contrast to the interpretation of the "Son of Man" as a messianic figure in other gospel works.

The Gospel of Mary emphasizes that the true self, represented by the "Son of Man," can only be found within. The "Son of Man" in the Gospel of Mary has roots in Platonic philosophy, where the existence of a Form of Man in the divine realm apart from particular humans was posited. The gospel interprets Jesus' teachings on the child of true humanity to refer to this archetypal form of man, in connection with the creation story in Genesis 1:26-27, where humanity is created in the image of God.

In the Gospel of Mary, the Savior uses the generic term "human being" and makes both Mary and the male disciples human beings. The Gospel of Mary strives to articulate a vision of a non-gendered divine and transcendent image, with sex and gender being seen as temporary and belonging to the lower sphere of bodily existence. The divine, in this gospel, is seen as nonmaterial and nongendered, represented only by the Good, a term that can easily be grammatically neutered. Conforming to the divine image, therefore, requires abandoning distinctions, including sex and gender, and embracing the spiritual and nongendered nature of the true self.

After the Savior left, Peter asks Mary to share any words of the Savior that she knew but were unknown to the other disciples (6:1-2). Mary reports a conversation she had with the Savior. She tells the Savior that she saw a vision of him and immediately acknowledged his presence. The Savior praised her for this and said, "Blessed are you for not wavering at seeing me. For where the mind is, there is the treasure" (7:3—4). This was an important statement as "wavering" implied instability of character. Mary's stability showed her conformity to the unchanging and eternal spiritual realm, demonstrating her advanced spiritual status. The saying about treasure is often quoted in early Christian literature. In Q, a collection of Jesus' words used by the writers of Matthew and Luke, the saying is used to warn people against greed and attachment to ephemeral wealth. In the Gospel of Mary, however, the saying introduces Mary's next question and points ahead to the Savior's response. She asks whether one receives a vision by the soul or the spirit. The Savior responds that "a person does not see with the soul or with the spirit. Rather the mind, which exists between these two, sees the vision and that is what . . . " Unfortunately, the text breaks off here. However, it is clear that he is describing the tripartite composition of the true inner self, made up of soul, mind, and spirit. Enough remains of the Savior's response to offer an intriguing answer to a difficult issue: how does a prophet see a vision? The mind conveys the vision, functioning as a mediator between the spirit and the soul.

Early Christians were fully a part of ancient Mediterranean society and shared the concepts common to that culture. They believed that gods and spirits communicated with people through trances, possessions, and dreams. Christians also had differing opinions on the matter, depending on which intellectual tradition they drew upon. In the Gospel of Mary, the Savior takes a specific position on the issue. The significance of his answer to Mary can be better appreciated by comparing it with the views of the church father Tertullian, who wrote A Treatise on the Soul (De anima) at the turn of the third century. Tertullian discussed this same issue but took a different position than the Gospel of Mary.

The Gospel of Mary valued prophetic experiences highly and considered them to be authoritative for Christian teaching and practice. They believed that only the pure could see God in visions because sin and attachment to the things of the flesh dimmed the spiritual comprehension of the soul. However, they disagreed on almost every other important issue. The most fundamental basis of their disagreement rested on conflicting views about what it means to be a human being. Tertullian understood a person to be made up of a body and soul, joined in a completely unified relationship. The mind was the ruling function of the soul, not something separate from it. He maintained that the soul, as well as the body, was material. The Gospel of Mary and Tertullian also differ in their understanding of prophetic experiences. Tertullian believed that prophecy occurred through the gift of the Holy Spirit, which was given to believers at baptism. He maintained that the Holy Spirit enabled the believer to speak in tongues, interpret Scripture, and receive revelations. For Tertullian, the prophetic gift was not limited to a select few but was available to all Christians. However, he also warned against false prophets and urged Christians to test the spirits to see if they were from God (1 John 4:1). In contrast, the Gospel of Mary views prophetic experiences as the result of the soul's purification and spiritual ascent. Only the pure and holy can see God in visions, and such experiences are not available to all but are given to a select few who have attained a high level of spiritual development.

The differences between Tertullian and the Gospel of Mary reflect broader debates within early Christianity about the nature of the self, the role of prophecy, and the relationship between the material and spiritual realms. These debates were influenced by Greek philosophy, Jewish mysticism, and Christian theology, and they shaped the development of Christian doctrine and practice. The Gospel of Mary provides a glimpse into one strand of early Christian thought, which emphasized the importance of inner spiritual transformation and valued the visionary experiences of the soul. While it is a fragmentary text and much of it remains unclear, it offers a unique perspective on the spiritual aspirations and concerns of early Christians.

Controversy over the Gospel of Mary

The Gospel of Mary mainly presents the teaching of the Savior, but it also contains a significant portion of conflict among the disciples. Before the Savior left, he commanded the disciples to preach the good news, but instead of immediately setting out, they were overwhelmed with distress and doubt. Mary comforted them and turned their thoughts to the Savior's words. Her words seemed to have restored harmony among the apostles. Later, Peter addressed Mary as their "sister" and asked her to share any teachings that the Savior may have given her. Mary agreed and gave them an extensive account of a vision and dialogue she had with the Lord. However, Andrew broke in with an accusatory challenge, denying that she could have received these teachings from the Savior because they seemed strange to him. Peter was even more contentious, questioning whether the Savior would have spoken to her in private without their knowledge. Peter apparently could not accept that the Savior would have withheld such advanced teaching from the male disciples and given it to a woman.

Mary's response to Peter's request apparently went far beyond his expectations. In the Coptic version, Mary really rubs it in: she says that she has teaching that has been hidden from them. The fact that she had received a vision further emphasizes her purity of heart and mind. The Savior himself acknowledged these qualities when he said, "How wonderful you are for not wavering at seeing me." Now Mary weeps, no doubt disturbed not only because Peter is suggesting that she has made everything up and is deliberately lying to her fellow disciples, but also because of the rivalry and animosity his words suggest. At this point, Levi steps in and rebukes Peter, telling him that if he persists, he will find himself on the side of their adversaries, the Powers, rather than on the side of the Savior. Levi reminds them that they should clothe themselves with the perfect Human and go forth to preach the gospel. With the departure of Levi or all the disciples, the gospel comes to an end.

This scene raises many questions. Did the disciples accept Levi's rebuke? Did they understand Mary's teaching? Were they able to work together again, or did they go off alone, harboring resentment and misunderstanding? We don't even know who left to go preach. Some versions of the story suggest that only Levi left. What about the others? Did they just stand there? Others suggest that "they" started going out to preach. But who was included in this "they"? Mary and Levi? Andrew and Peter? All the disciples? We don't know. The Gospel of Mary is not clear about what actually happened.

The Gospel of Mary seems to side with Mary and Levi against Andrew and Peter, but it's unclear why Mary's integrity is questioned at all if the work wishes to affirm her teaching. The ending is also ambiguous. Some commentators suggest that this scene reflects real conflicts that happened in second century Christianity. Others suggest that Peter and Mary (or Peter/Andrew and Mary/Levi) represent different positions under debate or different groups in conflict with each other. However, this solution raises more questions. Does the final scene in the Gospel of Mary reflect actual conflict between the historical figures of Peter and Mary? If so, what were the tensions about? Or were Peter and Mary (Andrew and Levi) only narrative representatives for opposing Christian groups or differing theological positions? If so, who were those groups? What positions did these figures represent? And what was at stake in the conflict?

The Gospel of Mary portrays most of the disciples as fearful and uncomprehending, even antagonistic, indicating that some of them have not understood the Savior's teaching. They are still caught up in the attachment to their bodies and appear to be still under the domination of the Powers who rule the world. They have not found the child of true Humanity within or conformed to the Image of the perfect Human. The attacks of Peter and Andrew on Mary demonstrate even more convincingly that they are still under the sway of passions and false opinions; they have failed to acquire inward peace, and out of jealousy and ignorance are sowing discord among the disciples. How can they preach the gospel of the Realm of the Human One if they do not themselves understand its message?

The Gospel of Mary has put in question the practice of basing authority solely on claims of having been the Savior's disciple and having received from him a commission to preach the gospel. Even being a witness to the resurrection does not appear to have been sufficient. The Gospel of Mary does, however, portray two disciples as reliable: Mary and Levi. Both work to bring unity and harmony to the group by calling the other disciples back to consideration of the words of the Savior. Mary, in particular, is portrayed as a model disciple, comforting the other disciples and offering advanced teaching from the Savior. Both her steadfastness and her vision of the Savior demonstrate the strength of her spiritual character. It is no accident that the Savior loved her more than the others; that love and esteem are based on his sure knowledge of her. More than any other disciple, she has comprehended the Savior's teaching and is capable of teaching and preaching the gospel to others. She shows no fear at the prospect of going forth to preach because she understands how the soul overcomes the passions and advances past the Powers that attempt to dominate it. The Gospel of Mary's portrayal of Mary and Levi makes it evident that demonstrable spiritual maturity is the crucial criterion for legitimate authority. The spiritual character of the persons who preach is the ultimate and most reliable basis for judging the truth of the gospel that is preached.

This criterion fits well with ancient expectations. Teachers were supposed to manifest their teaching in their actions, providing instruction not only by what they said but by how they lived. The personal character of the teacher was considered fundamental to his or her capacity to instruct. Women teachers of philosophy were known in antiquity, although they were few in number. We have to remember too that when the Gospel of Mary was written, no rule of faith or fixed canon had yet become commonly accepted. In the early centuries, Christians often based claims for the truth of their gospel on demonstrations of the power of the Spirit in prophecy and healing or in high standards of moral living. Thus representing the steadfast and irenic character of Mary and Levi would go a long way toward establishing the Gospel of Mary's authority.

The Gospel of Mary is mainly focused on challenges to its teachings by other apostles in the Christian community. If Andrew and Peter are any indication, these challenges were mainly two-fold: 1) rejection of new teachings based on prophecy or private revelation, and 2) gender. Other Christian writings from the first and second centuries indicate that these were real issues during that time. For example, Irenaeus denied that the apostles possessed hidden mysteries delivered to them in private, and he accused heretics of inventing and preaching their own fictions. In the Gospel of Mary, Peter's accusation against Mary implies that she made up everything she was reporting. Mary's character and Levi's defense support her against these charges. Levi's defense of Mary starts by attacking Peter's character, who was known to be a hot-head, sowing division among the apostles themselves. Levi then affirms that the Savior knew Mary completely and loved her best. The Gospel of Mary emphasizes the strength of Mary's relationship with the Savior to affirm her teachings.

The Savior's judgment of Mary is illustrated by the work's portrayal of her as an unflinching and steadfast disciple, worthy of receiving visions and advanced teaching. Levi's defense is not remarkable since the standards for legitimacy are those found widely in the earliest literature: apostolic witness to the resurrection and the demonstration of spiritual gifts, in Mary's case prophetic visions and inspired teaching. All apostles in the text can claim to be witnesses to Jesus' teaching ministry, both before and after his resurrection, and all received his commission to go forth and preach the gospel. Mary's qualifications are not sufficient to defend her from attacks by fellow apostles. The crux of the defense rests on the remarkable intimacy of Mary's relationship with the Savior. As Levi states, the Savior loved Mary more than the other disciples. Andrew's objection to the "strangeness" of Mary's teaching is never explicitly answered, leaving the issue for the reader to decide. There are multiple points of contact between the revelation to Mary and the Savior's earlier teachings; however, the reader must decide whether they are sufficient to exonerate her or not.

The second challenge to Mary's authority as a teacher and apostle concerns gender, explicitly raised in the text three times. Peter acknowledges that Jesus loved Mary more than the rest of women (GMary 6:1). Peter questions Mary's credibility, asking if Jesus spoke with her in private without their knowledge, and if they are to turn around and listen to her. He also questions if Jesus chose her over them (10:3-4). Levi responds, recognizing that Peter's problem had to do with Mary being a woman, and makes it clear that the Savior did indeed love her more and gave her special teaching because she, a woman, was worthy of it.

The issue of gender is not raised merely to score a point in the interminable battle of the sexes. Mary's gender is crucial to the Gospel of Mary's theology, especially the teaching about the body and salvation. For the Gospel of Mary, bodily distinctions are irrelevant to spiritual character since the body is not the true self. Just as God is non-gendered, immaterial, and transcendent, so too is the true human self. The Savior tells his disciples that they get sick and die "because you love what deceives you" (GMary 3:7-8). Peter's fault lies in his inability to see past the distinctions of the flesh to the spiritual qualities necessary for leadership. He apparently "loves" the status his male sex-gender gives him, leading to pride and jealousy. The scene where Levi corrects Peter's ignorance helps the reader to see one of the primary ways in which people are deceived by the body.

Authority should not be based on whether one is a man or a woman, let alone on roles of socially assigned gender and sexual reproduction, but on spiritual achievement. Those who have progressed further than others have the responsibility to care and instruct them. The claim to have known Jesus and heard his words was not enough. One had to have appropriated them in one's life. Leadership is for those who have sought and found the child of true Humanity; they are to point the way for others, even as the Savior did. And such persons can be women as well as men. According to the Gospel of Mary, those who fail to understand this fact are, like Peter, mired in the materiality and passions of their lower natures.

Worse yet, they risk finding themselves on the side of the Adversaries, for those who oppose women's spiritual leadership do so out of false pride, jealousy, lack of understanding, spiritual immaturity, and contentiousness.

Rejecting the body as the self opened up the possibility of an ungendered space within the Christian community in which leadership functions were based on spiritual maturity.

The Gospel of Mary takes two strong stances regarding the basis of authority. It suggests that spiritual maturity, demonstrated through prophetic experience and unwaveringness of mind, is more reliable than mere apostolic lineage in interpreting apostolic tradition. Additionally, it suggests that spiritual maturity, rather than an individual's gender, should form the basis for leadership. On these foundations, the Gospel claims to not only possess the true understanding of Jesus' teachings, but also to have a vision of Christian community and mission that reflects the Savior's own model as a teacher and mediator of salvation.

Furthermore, the Gospel presents an alternative to the sole reliance on apostolic witness as the source of authority. Although Mary knew the historical Jesus, witnessed the resurrection, and received instruction from the Savior, these experiences are not what distinguish her from the others. Throughout the Gospel, Mary is portrayed as an exemplary disciple. She does not falter when the Savior departs, but instead steps into his place, comforting, strengthening, and instructing the others. Her spiritual comprehension and maturity are demonstrated in her calm behavior and especially in her visionary experience. These experiences provide evidence of her spiritual maturity and form the basis for her legitimate exercise of authority in instructing the other disciples. She does not teach in her own name, but instead passes on the words of the Savior, calming the disciples and turning their hearts toward the Good. Her character proves the truth of her revelation and, by extension, authorizes the teaching of the Gospel of Mary. It does so by opposing those apostles who reject women's authority and preach another gospel, laying down laws beyond those that the Savior determined.

The Gospel and acceptance into early Christianity

The Gospel of Mary was written before the canon had been established. At that time, early Christians debated the meaning of Jesus' teachings and his importance for salvation. Jesus did not write, so all portraits of him reflect the perspectives of early Christians. Historians have spent centuries investigating how those portraits developed. They have constructed the following picture: Jesus said and did some things that were remembered and passed down orally. People did not repeat everything he said and did, but only what was particularly memorable or distinctive, especially what was of use in the early churches for preaching, teaching, ritual practices, and other aspects of community life. His parables and his sayings (called aphorisms) were often so striking that they were repeated again and again. For example, a saying like "Blessed are the poor," would have surely struck people as remarkable. In the process of being passed down, his words and deeds were interpreted and elaborated.

The Gospel of Matthew interpreted the saying about poverty allegorically: "Blessed are the poor in spirit" (Matt 5:3); while the Gospel of Luke read it as a pronouncement against injustices tied to wealth and greed: "But woe to you who are rich, for you have received your consolation" (Luke 6:24). Some materials were adapted to fit the needs of developing communities for worship or mission; others were elaborated to address new situations that arose. Some sayings attributed to Jesus in the gospels came from early Christian prophets who claimed to have received revealed teaching from the Lord in the Spirit. Traditions about Jesus were used and passed down primarily in oral form as part of the living practice of early Christians. Gradually various elements of oral tradition were frozen in writing, sometimes as a collection of Jesus' words like the Gospel of Thomas, sometimes in a narrative like the Gospel of Mark.

These writings give us glimpses of how the Jesus tradition was being used and interpreted by the earliest Christians, but it would be historically incorrect to think they reflect the full breadth of early Christian interpretation of that tradition. Recent discoveries like the Gospel of Mary and the Gospel of Thomas have started to fill in some gaps, but they also prove that theological reflections in the first centuries of Christian beginnings were much more diverse and varied than we had ever realized. Moreover, only a few of the many writings by early Christians have survived. Even if all the early Christian literature had been preserved, those written sources would represent only a fraction of the full story because the gospel was spread primarily by mouth and ear: it was preached and heard. Christian ideas and practices developed in the primarily oral contexts of evangelizing, prayer and worship, preaching and prophesying.

Furthermore, the written gospels did not play the same role in early Christian life that they have in our own literate, print societies. People in ancient times were often suspicious of books. When Irenaeus argued for the authority of the four gospels in the late second century, he had to counter the views of Christians who claimed that "truth was not transmitted by means of written documents, but in living speech." True teaching was communicated directly through speech, and the most powerful and authoritative kind of speech was prophetic revelation. As the literary sources that have survived were copied and passed on, they were sometimes altered to suit new situations and theological demands. A striking example of this can be seen in the relationships among the gospels of Matthew, Mark, and Luke. The majority of scholars maintain that the authors of Luke and Matthew knew the Gospel of Mark and adapted it to fit their interpretations of Jesus' teaching and ministry. Materials could easily be added on to the end of works, like the final saying in the Gospel of Thomas (114) or the longer ending to the Gospel of Mark (16:9-20), to say nothing of both intentional and accidental changes that undoubtedly occurred in the process of manually copying the manuscripts. By the beginning of the second century, these processes had resulted in a highly diverse body of gospel material, all claiming to present the words and deeds of Jesus.

Comparison of the Gospel of Mary with other Gospel books

Paul

The Gospel of Mary has similarities with Paul's letters in terms of vocabulary and concepts. Ann Pasquier believes that Romans 7 is closely tied to Gospel of Mary 3-4.1.

GMary 3:3-8, 10-13 explains that the Savior said, "Sin doesn't exist; instead, you create sin when you act according to the nature of adultery, which is called 'sin.' For this reason, the Good came among you, pursuing what every nature deserves. It will set it within its root." Then he continued, saying, "This is why you get sick and die: because you love what deceives you. . . . Matter gave birth to a passion which has no image because it comes from what's against nature. A disturbing confusion then occurred in the whole body. That's why I told you, 'Be content at heart, but also remain discontent and disobedient; in fact, be content and agreeable only in the presence of the other image of nature.'"

GMary 4:9-10 says, "Don't make any rules beyond what I decided for you, nor create any laws like the lawgiver, or else you may be dominated by them."

Romans 7:1-8, 22-23 reads, "Do you not know, brethren—for I am speaking to those who know the law—that the law is binding on a person only during one's life? Thus a married woman is bound by law to her husband as long as he lives; but if her husband dies she is discharged from the law concerning the husband. Accordingly, she will be called an adulteress if she lives with another man when her husband is alive. But if her husband dies she is free from that law, and if she marries another man she is not an adulteress. Likewise, my brethren, you have died to the law through the body of Christ, so that you may belong to another, to him who has been raised from the dead in order that we may bear fruit for God.

While we were living in the flesh, our sinful passions, aroused by the law, were at work in our members to bear fruit for death. But now we are discharged from the law, dead to that which held us captive, so that we serve not under the old written code but in the new life of the Spirit. What then shall we say? That the law is sin? By no means! Yet if it had not been for the law, I would not have known sin. I would not have known what coveting is if the law had not said, 'You shall not covet.' But sin, finding opportunity in the commandment, wrought in me all kinds of covetousness. Apart from the law sin lies dead. ... For I delight in the law of God in my inmost self, but I see in my members another law at war with the law of my mind and making me captive to the law of sin which dwells in my members."

Pasquier lists the following points of agreement between these passages:

*   The law's domination is compared to adultery.
*   Adultery is compared to enslavement to passion and it leads to death.
*   Freedom from the law means overcoming domination by death.
*   Sin doesn't actually exist.
*   Law, sin, and death are interconnected.
*   An opposition is made between the divine law/nature which gives life and that fleshly law/nature which imprisons or dominates one.

According to Pasquier, the Gospel of Mary placed Paul's discussion of law into a cosmological context, transforming his attempt to understand the value of Jewish law in light of Christ's death and resurrection. This shift greatly alters the meaning of Paul's message. While Paul argues that Christ came to free humanity from sin, the Savior in the Gospel of Mary warns against adulterous attachment to the material world and the body. Unlike Paul, the Gospel of Mary does not see law as divine and purposeful (Rom 7:7, 12-14), but as a tool of domination.

It is unclear whether the author of the Gospel of Mary intentionally used this passage from Paul to change its message. There are no direct quotes, and the language and themes of passion, sin, adultery, law, and death are present in a variety of literature.

Since Paul's letters were being circulated widely by the second century, it is possible that readers connected the two works due to their similarities. The important issue is not whether the Gospel of Mary was influenced by Paul, but how reading the two works together would affect their meanings and theological impact.

In Romans 7-8, Paul writes to fellow Christians in Rome about how Gentiles can receive salvation through faith in Christ. His argument is centered around how they can overcome the carnal desires and passions which enslave them, and how they refuse to acknowledge the true God. Paul argues that they cannot overcome these sinful passions through the law, but only through faith in Christ's death and resurrection (or through Christ's faithfulness) can they serve God in the new life of the Spirit. The reference to adultery serves to illustrate the legal status of Gentiles before God.

In GMary 3, Jesus raises the themes of sin, adultery, and death in response to Peter's question, "What is the sin of the world?" Paul's concern for the admission of Gentiles into the community of Israel is not at issue. Instead, the problem is how to understand and overcome human enslavement to passion in view of the material nature of the body and the world. For the Gospel of Mary, sin is not a matter of right and wrong actions. Rather, it has to do with the improper mixing (adultery) of material and spiritual natures, which leads to the improper domination of the spiritual nature by the material. Salvation is achieved by overcoming attachment to the body and the material world, for it is this attachment which keeps people enslaved to suffering and death.

Both Paul and the Gospel of Mary have been misunderstood. Paul's insistence on faith as the sole route to salvation does not mean that the ethical life is not important, as the author of the Letter of James argues.

Paul and the Gospel of Mary address the issue of how to overcome sin and death. They have a similar diagnosis of the problem, that desires and passions lead to death, and a similar solution, that the life of the spirit is the key.

126

However, they differ because their views of sin and salvation are focused on different concerns and contexts. For Paul, the main issue is the relation of Gentiles to the Jewish law in the face of Christ's saving death and resurrection. In contrast, the Gospel of Mary focuses on understanding the Savior's teaching about the nature of sin and the means of overcoming suffering and death.

The actual behaviors of those who followed these two views appeared very similar, but the two groups would have understood the meaning of their behaviors quite differently. Individuals who embrace the principles presented in texts such as the Gospel of Mary or the letters of Paul have their ethical reasoning guided by the worldview and values espoused in the literature. These works not only depict reality but also present ideals of what should be. They furnish frameworks of significance that enable ethical deliberation and promote congruent conduct. Accordingly, the tales we recount and the literature we cherish play an essential role in developing our moral imagination and sentiment. The kind of narratives we are exposed to hold great importance.

The work of Paul and the Gospel of Mary provide very different orientations for thinking about what it means to be a human being. For Paul, the self is a physical, psychic, and spiritual whole. The body is thus fully part of the self, even as the soul is. Paul believed that people without faith perish at death, body and soul. There is no hint of the idea of an immortal life of punishment for unbelievers. When men die, they stay dead. Believers, on the other hand, rise to immortal life with God. The physical body is transformed into a spiritual body, immortal and freed from all mortal passions and suffering. For Paul, moral behavior is essential in purifying the body so that it can be the spiritual dwelling place of God, not in overcoming the attachment of the soul to the body, as in the Gospel of Mary.

For the Gospel of Mary, the body is not one's true self. Only the soul infused with the spirit carries the truth of what it means to be a human being. As a result, the ethical concern is focused not on catering to the desires of the body, but on strengthening the spiritual self. At death, the liberated soul is released from the body and ascends to rest with God beyond time and eternity, while the corpse returns to the inanimate material nature from which it came.

Gospel of John

In comparing the Gospel of Mary and the Gospel of John, we can see that both works focus on the role of Mary of Magdala. In John's Gospel, Jesus comforts his disciples before his departure and tells them to bear witness to the truth, even though they will face persecution. In the Gospel of Mary, Mary steps in to comfort the frightened disciples and reminds them that the Savior's grace will be with them. Both works affirm that the Savior has prepared and united his followers so that they are ready to face what he commanded them to do.

The Gospel of Mary does not assign blame to the Jews, and the disciples' fear follows the Savior's commission to go out and preach. However, Mary's message about her vision of the Savior makes it clear that not all the disciples have understood the Savior's teaching and not all are prepared to preach the gospel. Mary alone is presented as ready and able to step into the Savior's role.

While the Gospel of John affirms Mary's role as a teacher to the other disciples, their portrayals exhibit significant differences. John states that the first appearance of the resurrected Lord was to Mary, and that she was the first to use the confessional title "Lord" to refer to him. However, Mary's status is diminished in the Gospel of John in that she at first mistakes him for the gardener, and then addresses him as "Teacher" (Rabboni), indicating a relatively low standing on the hierarchical scale of Johannine Christological titles.

In the Gospel of Mary, Mary immediately recognizes the Lord when he appears and he praises her for her steadfastness of mind. She takes over many of his roles after his departure and is consistently portrayed as a model disciple and apostle. Mary's weeping is not a sign of weakness, but compassion, demonstrating her distress at both the disciples' lack of comprehension and their fomenting of discord among the apostles. In the end, Levi's speech offers a decisive defense of Mary, entirely vindicating her. The Gospel of Mary is the only text where Mary actually gets to speak in her own defense.

The Apostles

The Gospel of Mary mentions four apostles by name: Levi, Andrew, Peter, and Mary. These individuals have become legendary figures in Christianity, inspiring countless works of art and literature. Despite their immense popularity, however, we have little reliable historical information about them. The ancient evidence regarding their lives and personalities is limited. In ancient literature, the apostles are not represented as unique individuals with distinctive psychological profiles and particular biographies, but rather as types. The writers of the gospels used the apostles as malleable characters to serve their own narrative purposes. For example, in the Gospel of Mark the apostles are often portrayed as misunderstanding Jesus, which gives him the opportunity to clarify his teachings. In other works, such as the Gospel of Luke, the apostles are depicted as faithful witnesses who can attest to Jesus' teachings and deeds.

While we must acknowledge the limited historical information available, it is important to remember that these four apostles were real people who followed Jesus during his travels through Galilee and up to Jerusalem. They were all Jews, and each had a specific background: Levi was a tax collector, Andrew and Peter were brothers who worked as fishermen, and Mary was from Magdala and was the first to have a vision of the Lord. Peter also saw the risen Christ and was a key leader in the early mission.

The apostles' prestige and popularity have obscured their historical reality with myth, legend, and ritual. Nevertheless, we should strive to understand what we can about these early followers of Jesus while recognizing the limitations of the ancient evidence.

Both the gospels of Mark and Luke depict Levi as a tax collector who became a follower of Jesus (Mark 2:14; Luke 5:27-29), but neither of them mentions him in their enumeration of the twelve disciples. In the Gospel of Matthew, however, there is a narrative about a tax collector (Matt 9:9), whose name is Matthew and who is listed as one of the twelve (Matt 10:3).

This ambiguity later resulted in a tradition that sometimes identified the two, but it is not evident that Levi was commonly considered one of the twelve in the early tradition. The Gospel of John does not mention him at all. In the second-century Gospel of Philip, a certain Levi is mentioned, but he is identified only as the owner of a dye works and is unlikely to be connected to the Levi who was a tax collector (GPhil 63:26). Levi also appears in the First Apocalypse of James 37:7, but the text is so fragmentary that it is hard to draw any conclusions about his role. Therefore, it is somewhat unexpected that Levi emerges as Mary's defender in the Gospel of Mary. Could he have been selected for this task because, like Mary, he was not one of the twelve, even though he was an early disciple of Jesus? It is difficult to determine. Nonetheless, in the Gospel of Mary, he is second only to Mary in understanding the Savior's teachings. He reprimands Peter and defends Mary's character, urging the apostles to return to the Savior's instructions and to preach the gospel. In the Greek fragment, only he departs to spread the good news.

Andrew's primary claim to fame is that he was the brother of Peter, and in the earliest literature, he appears almost solely in that context. In the Gospel of Mark, he and Peter are portrayed as fishermen from Capernaum, the first of the disciples called by the Lord (Mark 1:16-18), and Andrew appears regularly in the lists of disciples in the Gospels (e.g., Mark 3:18; Matt 10:2; Luke 6:14; Acts 1:13). In the Gospel of John, he appears initially as a follower of John the Baptist, but becomes the first disciple called by Jesus and leads his brother Peter to the Lord as well (John 1:35-42). He is the only apostle mentioned by name in the surviving portion of the newly discovered Gospel of the Savior, but unfortunately, his words are lost in a gap (GSav 97:31-32).' His only other appearance in the early literature is in the Gospel of Mary, where again he appears in close conjunction with Peter and is quickly overshadowed by his brother's presence. Andrew's complaint against Mary receives no direct response either from her or from Levi, both of whom address only Peter. Andrew does not appear again in Christian literature until the end of the second century, when he becomes the hero of the Acts of Andrew, a massive work that portrays him as a miracle-working missionary sent to Achaea, northern Anatolia, Thrace, and Macedonia.

There he is active in breaking up marriages by preaching celibacy and is crucified by an enraged husband on the shore of the sea. Eventually, Andrew takes a firm place in Christian legend as the apostolic guarantor of the bishop's see of Byzantium, where his role of bringing Peter to the faith becomes a most useful tool in the polemics between Byzantium and Rome over ecclesiastical supremacy. All of this, however, occurs long after the Gospel of Mary was written, and there is no hint that the author would expect readers to associate anything with Andrew except his fraternal tie to Peter.

Historically, Peter, also known as Simon and Cephas (Mark 3:16; Matt 10:2; 16:17-19), was a fisherman from Capernaum on the Sea of Galilee (Mark 1:16-18). He accompanied Jesus throughout his ministry and was a prominent member of the inner circle of his followers. Peter was married, and it appears that his wife traveled with him on missionary journeys throughout Asia Minor (Mark 1:29-31; 1 Cor 15:5). There is some dispute about later tradition, which reports that he was martyred and buried in Rome—usually along Catholic-Protestant lines.

Peter plays a significant role in early Christian literature, and Levi's remark implying that Peter's temper and impetuosity were well-known indicates clearly that readers would be expected to know something of the tradition about him. Peter's role in the Gospel of Mary has struck some scholars as revisionary, for here Peter does not appear as the illustrious rock upon which Jesus founded the church, but rather as an ignorant hothead who sowed discord among the disciples. However, this portrait has a strong basis in early Christian tradition, a tradition that painted Peter as a complex and ambiguous character.

The Gospel of Mark, for example, recounts a scene where Jesus himself called Peter "Satan" (Mark 8:31-33): Jesus had just predicted his death and suffering, and Peter had the audacity to tell Jesus he was wrong! Once Jesus had to save Peter from drowning because his faith was too weak to walk on water (Matt 14:29-31).

At the transfiguration, his fear leads him to offer to build three booths, one each for Moses, Elijah, and Jesus (Mark 9:5-6). Still later, Peter insisted that even if everyone else abandoned Jesus, he would never do so—and this just before he denies him not once, but three times (Mark 14:29-31; 66-72), a story recounted not only in Mark, but also in the other canonical gospels. In another scene in the Gospel of John, Peter initially refuses to have Jesus wash his feet; but when Jesus says that otherwise Peter will have no part in him, Peter goes overboard in the other direction and demands that Jesus wash his hands and head as well (John 13:6-11).

In Gethsemane, when the disciples fall asleep while Jesus prays, Jesus' disappointment is directed primarily at Peter: "Simon, are you asleep? Could you not watch one hour? Watch and pray that you may not enter into temptation; the spirit indeed is willing, but the flesh is weak" (Mark 14:37-38). At the arrest, Peter pulls out a sword and cuts off the ear of the high priest's slave Malchus, earning another rebuke from Jesus (John 18:10-11). As noted earlier, even Paul had difficulties with Peter and accused him of being a hypocrite by changing his behavior to suit his audience (Gal 2:11-13). These repeated examples in the early literature consistently portray Peter as a bold fellow, but also as someone who doesn't quite understand what is going on. The Gospel of the Nazarenes took a very harsh position on Peter's character and pronounced the final judgment that Peter "denied and swore and damned himself (GNaz 19).

Peter is often characterized in a certain way, but he is also attributed to many early Christian works, such as the canonical letters of 1 and 2 Peter, the Gospel of Peter, the Letter of Peter to Philip, the Apocalypse of Peter, the Kerygma Petri, and the Acts of Peter. Although these works consistently portray Peter positively as a guarantor of apostolic authority, he remains theologically ambiguous. This is because he is used to legitimize conflicting theological positions. For example, 2 Peter claims explicit support for apostolic authority from Peter and invokes his authority against certain interpretations of Paul that the author of the letter opposed.

While Irenaeus cites Peter as a witness to the physical reality of Jesus' incarnation, the Apocalypse of Peter has him receive a revelation from the Savior that denies the incarnation and affirms that Jesus only appeared to have a body. In the Gospel of Peter, Peter appears only once in the extant fragment, but in a crucial role. The manuscript breaks off here, and what happened afterward is unknown. Still, it is highly likely that it was an account of the first resurrection appearance of Jesus.

After the second century, Peter continued to have a long and illustrious legacy in legend, art, and ecclesiastical politics as the foremost apostle of Christian faith, the co-founder of the Roman church, and the apostolic guarantor for papal authority. However, in the Gospel of Mary, Peter appears solely in his role as an ignorant hothead. His challenge to Mary presents him as a jealous man who cannot see past the weakness of the flesh to discern spiritual truth.

The earliest Christian texts, including the gospels in the New Testament, portray Mary of Magdala as a noteworthy Jewish follower of Jesus of Nazareth. Her name "Magdalene" suggests that she came from the town of Magdala (Migdal), which is located on the west coast of the Sea of Galilee (Lake Gennesaret), just north of Tiberias. Alongside other women, she went with Jesus during his ministry, was present at his crucifixion and burial, and witnessed the empty tomb. Mary of Magdala is given a significant position among Jesus' followers, particularly the women followers, in the early Christian gospel traditions. She is often listed first among the women who followed Jesus, and she is one of the main speakers in several texts from the first and second centuries that record post-resurrection dialogues between Jesus and his disciples. In the Gospel of John, the risen Jesus gives her specific instructions and commissions her to announce the good news of the resurrection to the other disciples, making her the first to proclaim the resurrection. Although Mary of Magdala is not directly referred to as an apostle, she fulfills the role, and later tradition hails her as "the apostle to the apostles." This literary tradition, attested to by multiple independent sources, suggests that Mary may have been a prophetic visionary and leader within some sector of the early Christian movement after Jesus' death.

134

The Gospel of Luke provides two additional details about Mary, but their historical accuracy is uncertain. Luke 8:2 identifies Mary as the one "from whom seven demons had gone out," but this is the only source to do so. Luke 8:3 mentions that Mary was financially independent and supported Jesus with her own resources, but this information may have been added at a later time when Christianity was supported by wealthy patrons. If accurate, it indicates that Mary had significant resources and was a patron of Jesus.

The Sophia of Jesus Christ, also from the second century, gives Mary a clear role as one of the seven women and twelve men gathered to hear the Savior after the resurrection, but before his ascension. Of these only five are named and speak, including Mary. At the end of his discourse, he tells them, "I have given you authority over all things as children of light," and they go forth in joy to preach the gospel. Mary is included among those special disciples to whom Jesus entrusted his most elevated teaching, and she is commissioned along with the other disciples to preach the gospel.

In the third-century text Pistis Sophia, Mary is portrayed as a prominent disciple. She asks more questions than all the rest of the disciples combined, and the Savior acknowledges that "You are she whose heart is more directed to the Kingdom of heaven than all your brothers." Mary is an active and vocal participant, with complete spiritual comprehension, who even steps in and intercedes with the Savior when the other disciples are in despair. Other narratives also portray Mary as a significant disciple.

In the Gospel of Philip, Mary Magdalene is explicitly mentioned as one of three Marys. The author wants readers to see that these figures are more than literal, historical characters. Mary is the image of a greater spiritual truth. Scholars have suggested different interpretations of this passage, based in large part on a later damaged section of the work. The Savior's intimate relationship with Mary is described, and Mary is also identified with Wisdom. The portrayal affirms the special relationship of Mary Magdalene to Jesus based on her spiritual perfection.

However, due to the limited historical information available, it is important to remember that these early followers of Jesus were real people who followed him during his travels through Galilee and up to Jerusalem. The gospels used the apostles as malleable characters to serve their own narrative purposes, and the apostles are not represented as unique individuals with distinctive psychological profiles and particular biographies, but rather as types.

Peter, who accompanied Jesus throughout his ministry and was a prominent member of the his inner circle of followers, is often characterized in a certain way, but he is also attributed to many early Christian works. Although these works consistently portray Peter positively as a guarantor of apostolic authority, he remains theologically ambiguous. This is because he is used to legitimizing conflicting theological positions.

Mary of Magdala, who is given a significant position among Jesus' followers in the early Christian gospel traditions, may have been a prophetic visionary and leader within some sectors of the early Christian movement after Jesus' death. Nevertheless, her historical accuracy is uncertain, and the information provided about her in the Gospel of Luke may have been added at a later time when Christianity was supported by wealthy patrons. For this reason, we should strive to understand what we can about these early followers of Jesus while recognizing the limitations of the ancient evidence.

Mary Magdalene is often portrayed as an exemplary disciple, but this positive symbolization of the feminine is not always consistent. It's important to note that even texts that emphasize her prominence can portray her as a controversial figure. For example, in the second-century Dialogue of the Savior, Mary is praised as "a woman who had understood completely." However, women are categorically associated with sexuality, and the works of womanhood are condemned. This hardly works to promote the status of women. Some scholars have different opinions on this passage, but Mary's response can also be read as resistance: the works of womanhood will never be obliterated.

In the Gospel of Thomas, Simon Peter wishes to exclude Mary simply because she is a woman. However, Jesus defends Mary's spiritual status by suggesting that her womanhood is not a permanent impediment to salvation. In a symbol system where "female" codes body, sexuality, and materiality, and "male" codes mind and spirit, to "become male" means that women are expected to transcend their naturally lower material natures and become spiritual beings. Jesus' statement destabilizes the categorical fixity of gender, but at best only moderates Peter's categorical sexism: women as women are not worthy of life; they need to become male.

It's important to note that while Mary Magdalene is lauded in these works, there are signs that she is becoming a center around which controversy swirls. The limited historical information available makes it challenging to draw any conclusions about Mary's role. Nonetheless, it's clear that Mary of Magdala is given a significant position among Jesus' followers, particularly the women followers, in the early Christian gospel traditions. She is often listed first among the women who followed Jesus and is one of the main speakers in several texts from the first and second centuries that record post-resurrection dialogues between Jesus and his disciples.

It's crucial to remember that these early followers of Jesus were real people who followed him during his travels through Galilee and up to Jerusalem. The gospels used the apostles as malleable characters to serve their own narrative purposes, and the apostles are not represented as unique individuals with distinctive psychological profiles and particular biographies, but rather as types. Peter, for instance, who accompanied Jesus throughout his ministry and was a prominent member of the inner circle of his followers, is often characterized in a certain way, but he is also attributed to many early Christian works. Although these works consistently portray Peter positively as a guarantor of apostolic authority, he remains theologically ambiguous. This is because he is used to legitimizing conflicting theological positions.

While there is limited historical information available, we should strive to understand what we can about these early followers of Jesus while recognizing the limitations of the ancient evidence. We should also be careful not to appropriate these works uncritically as feminist resources simply on the basis of a positive portrayal of Mary, for they can also employ feminine imagery that denigrates femaleness.

In the third-century work Pistis Sophia, Peter and Mary are shown in conflict. Mary, the most outspoken disciple in this work, wants to offer her interpretation of what has been said, but she complains that Peter threatens her and hates their race (PiSo II. 71:2). The Lord defends Mary by affirming that no power can prevent anyone filled with the Spirit of light from interpreting the things being said. However, the response is less than ideal for women. Although Mary has accused Peter of misogyny, the Savior's response does not condemn him but simply explains that anyone who is "filled with the Spirit of light," man or woman, has the capacity and the responsibility to speak. The point is that sex and gender are irrelevant to spiritual development. While the Pistis Sophia recognizes the superiority of Mary's spiritual understanding, it relegates the tasks of preaching the gospels solely to the male disciples.

The Gospel of Mary belongs to the same tradition as the figure of Mary in portraying her as a prominent disciple. However, more than any other early Christian text, it presents an unflinchingly favorable portrait of her as a woman leader among the disciples. Mary is the most prominent character and is portrayed as the ideal disciple and apostle. She is the only one who does not fear for her life at the departure of the Lord. The Savior himself praises her for her unwavering steadfastness. She is favored with a special vision of Jesus and receives advanced teaching about the fate of the soul and salvation. She comforts and instructs the other disciples, turning their attention toward the teaching of Jesus and toward the divine Good. While her teaching does not go unchallenged, in the end both the truth of her teachings and her authority to teach the male disciples are affirmed. She is portrayed as a prophetic visionary and as a leader among the disciples.

But this portrait of Mary is not the only one, as we all know. In Western European art and literature, Mary Magdalene is most often portrayed as a repentant prostitute, the Christian model of female sexuality redeemed. She stands prominently with two other figures: Eve, the temptress whose sin brought all of humanity under the judgment of death and all women into just subjugation and obedience, and Mary, the virgin mother whose impossible sexuality both idealizes and frustrates the desires of real women. Together they have formed the three-legged base upon which normative Christian models of female identity are balanced.

Where did this portrait of Mary Magdalene as a repentant whore come from? Contrary to popular Western tradition, Mary Magdalene was never a prostitute. Eastern Orthodox traditions have never portrayed her as one. She appears in the Gospel of Mary in a role closer to her actual position in early Christian history: an early and important disciple of Jesus and a leader in the early Christian movement. As with most of the other disciples, the very meagerness of what was known about Mary's life served only to fire the imaginations of later Christians, who elaborated her history in story and art according to their spiritual needs and political aims.

In contrast to the prominent role she plays in the early literature we have just discussed, the early church fathers whose writings later become the basis for orthodoxy largely ignore Mary Magdalene. When they do mention her, however, they present her in a consistently favorable light. She is usually mentioned to support points they are trying to make about the reality of the physical resurrection or the nature of the soul. Her name comes up most frequently in connection with the resurrected Jesus' enigmatic statement to her: "Do not touch me, for I have not yet ascended to the Father" (John 20:17). The fathers were concerned to counter any implication in this passage that Jesus' resurrection might not have been physical. Their concern was not unfounded, since the passage belongs to the earliest appearance narratives which were based on visionary experiences, not on encounters with a resuscitated corpse.

No criticism was directed at Mary Magdalene for Jesus' reticence about letting Mary touch him. Indeed, Tertullian praised Mary because she approached Jesus to touch him "out of love, not from curiosity, nor with Thomas' incredulity." In Tertullian's mind, the issue was simply that it was too early for touching; the resurrection had to be completed by Jesus' ascent.

From the fourth century onward, there was a clear shift in tone among the fathers, who began to have difficulty with Mary Magdalene's portrayal in the gospels. However, they confidently resolved this by creating a different understanding of her character. They argued that Mary was not worthy of touching the resurrected Lord because she lacked a full understanding of the resurrection and hence lacked true faith. She was sent to the male apostles, not to proclaim the good news of the resurrection, but rather so that her weakness could be supplemented by their strength. By conflating the account of the Gospel of John with that of the Gospel of Matthew 28:9, which tells of an appearance to at least two women, Origen confidently argued that Mary was not alone in seeing the risen Lord. The effect was to de-emphasize Mary's status as the first witness to the resurrection by making her only one member of a group. Nonetheless, the fathers confidently argued that it was appropriate for a woman to be the first to receive the redemption offered by Jesus through his resurrection, because, after all, it was a woman who had first brought sin into the world. Mary Magdalene was referred to as the second Eve, the woman whose faith in the resurrected Jesus overcame the offenses of the first Eve.

The private instruction that Mary received from the risen Jesus was a difficult problem. By the end of the second century, she had become closely associated with an interpretation of Jesus' teachings that was very different from what the church fathers were developing. The Gospel of Mary presents such teachings, and the content and the tide of the work associate these "heretical" views with Mary. Discrediting her may therefore have been in part a confident strategy of the church fathers to counter the interpretation of Jesus being spread in works like the Gospel of Mary.

It turned out that silence was not an effective strategy, since it left the imaginative field open to others. So starting in the fourth century, Christian theologians in the Latin West confidently began to construct an alternative story. The first move was to associate Mary Magdalene with the unnamed sinner who anointed Jesus' feet in Luke 7:36-50. Further confusion resulted by conflating the account in John 12:1-8, in which Mary of Bethany anoints Jesus, with the anointing by the unnamed woman in the Lukan account. From this point, identifying Mary of Magdala with Mary of Bethany was but a short step. At the end of the sixth century, Pope Gregory the Great confidently gave a sermon in which he not only identified these figures, but drew a moral conclusion that would dominate the imagination of the West for centuries to come: that Mary was the woman whom Luke calls the sinful woman, whom John calls Mary, and we believe to be the Mary from whom seven devils were ejected according to Mark. The overall picture sketched above accurately reflects the issues at stake and the positions that the church fathers took on those issues. Notably, the Eastern Churches never confused any of these Marys with unnamed prostitutes or adulteresses.

Mary Magdalene fell into the patriarchal trap of being defined primarily by her sexual roles and her relations to men, as virgins, wives, and mothers, widows, or prostitutes. As the symbolic field of the virgin and mother was already held by another Mary, and our Mary was not known to have been married or widowed, that left only the prostitute option available. It is safe to say that if Mary Magdalene had not been figured in this role, some other character would necessarily have been invented to play it. Its symbolic significance was too great to ignore.

Early on, the possibility existed that Mary Magdalene might emerge from the speculative fray as Jesus' wife and lover. The Gospel of Philip said that Jesus used to kiss her often, and in the Gospel of Mary, Peter affirmed that Jesus loved her more than other women. The third-century church father Hippolytus also used erotic imagery to allegorize the Song of Songs into an intimate relationship of the Church to Christ by treating Mary of Magdala as the Church-Bride and Jesus as the Savior-Bridegroom.

Of course, the rise of celibacy to a position of central importance in determining Christian authority structures put an official damper on these kinds of speculations. Still, the notion of an erotic relationship between Jesus and Mary Magdalene has surfaced at odd moments throughout Western history and is still capable of arousing a good deal of public ire.

Yet the role of the repentant prostitute is symbolically appealing in its own right, and not just because the other options were closed off. It has proven itself to be a much more evocative figure than that of Mary as Jesus' wife or lover. The image of Mary as the redeemed sinner has nourished a deep empathy that resonates with our human imperfection, frailty, and mortality. A fallen redeemer figure has enormous power to redeem. She holds out the possibility that purity and wholeness are never closed off; that redemption is always a possibility at hand. Despite the appropriation of sinful female sexuality for patriarchal aims, her rich tradition in story and art attests to the redemptive power of the repentant sinner.

And indeed, Mary Magdalene has been a figure of importance not just for patriarchy, where too often Gregory's praise of a woman who "immolated herself" in order to burn out "every delight she had had in herself has resulted in untold anguish, physical abuse, and self-destruction. Nonetheless, women are not only victims, but like all people are agents of their own lives, and so women have often interpreted her in ways that were unanticipated and no doubt not entirely welcomed. From the second to the twenty-first century, women prophets and preachers have continued to appeal to her to legitimate their own leadership roles.

The fact is that both women and men in Western society lack the option of an unambiguous symbolic tradition to draw upon. A confluence of historical tradition with various theological problems, patriarchal prejudices, and human affections converged to result in the complex portrait of Mary Magdalene as a repentant prostitute and preacher. The portrait was sustained over the centuries and flourished because of even more complex motives and aims.

142

In the end, two basic portraits of Mary Magdalene developed, each with many variations: one stressed her roles as a prominent disciple of Jesus, a visionary, and a spiritual teacher; the other painted her as a repentant prostitute whom Jesus forgave, a latter-day Eve turned from her sinful ways. While both portraits have legendary aspects, only the first has any claim to historical truth. The portrait of Mary as a repentant prostitute is pure fiction with no historical foundation whatsoever. The historical Mary of Magdala was a prominent Jewish follower of Jesus, a visionary, and a leading apostle.

The History of Christianity

So far, every analysis of the Gospel of Mary has classified it as a text belonging to the second-century heresy called Gnosticism. However, there was no religion in antiquity called Gnosticism. Scholars invented the term in the process of categorizing the variety of early Christian heresies. As we said above, they divided the earliest types into two groups: Jewish Christianity and Gnosticism. Jewish Christianity is characterized by too much or too positive an appropriation of "Judaism"; Gnosticism by too little "Judaism" or too negative an attitude toward it. Orthodoxy is just right, rejecting "Jewish error" but claiming the heritage of Scripture for its own. This typology establishes the "correct" relationship to Jewish Scripture and tradition as the single most important factor in defining normative Christian identity. These types, however, can be established only by hindsight, and even then they are not real entities, but only academic constructs. In other words, all the texts and persons grouped under these categories did exist in antiquity, but they never understood themselves to be Gnostics or Jewish Christians, let alone heretics. Calling them Gnostics is simply a shorthand method for labeling them as heretics while maintaining the appearance of impartiality. It disguises the degree to which normative interests have pervaded supposedly objective and disinterested scholarship. I never call the Gospel of Mary a Gnostic text because there was no such thing as Gnosticism.

It is true that all early Christians argued for the truth of their own theology and practice over against competing claims, but if we start out by dividing these groups into winners and losers, orthodoxy and heresy, it becomes impossible to see how early Christianity was really shaped. As I said above, this procedure obscures the complex dynamics of early Christian theology-making because it tends to treat all the "orthodox" texts primarily in terms of their similarities to each other and their differences from heresy, a procedure that obscures the real diversity of the New Testament literature and the processes by which the Nicene Creed and the canon were shaped.

So, too, the enormous theological variety of the literature classified as Gnostic gets harmonized into an overly simplified and distorting monolithic ideology. This procedure makes it appear that all Gnostic texts say more or less the same thing and permits their theology to be explained primarily in terms of how it deviates from the orthodox norm.

On the other hand, when historians set aside the anachronistic classification of early Christian literature into orthodox and heretical forms, analyzing both the similarities and the differences among the extant remains, then a much more complex picture emerges. It becomes possible to consider afresh what was at stake in how Christians formulated their beliefs and practices, and we come to see more clearly the dynamics of their interactions and the nature of the debates in which they were engaged. Eliminating these anachronistic terms of theological hindsight fosters a fundamental rethinking of the formation of early Christianity. Contemporary Christians may gain new insights and resources for reflecting on what it means to be a Christian in a pluralistic world and for addressing the pressing need to rethink the relationship of Christianity to Judaism, Islam, and other religious traditions in order to meet the demands for social well-being and justice.

We can begin by considering how the master story of Christianity has been constructed. Although Jesus and his earliest followers lived in the first century, Christianity as we know it was forged in the second to fourth centuries. These are the centuries in which creed and canon were shaped, in which the idea of the New Testament as a collection of books came into being, in which creedal statements gradually came into use as gauges of correct belief. First-century Christians had no New Testament or Nicene Creed. For most observers, this well-known fact has not seemed problematic; and since early Christians wrote and distributed these works, the New Testament texts and early creeds are indeed important primary source materials for the reconstruction of the history of early Christianity. Yet so fundamental are creed and canon to informing our very definition of what Christianity is that it is almost impossible to imagine what Christianity was like without them.

As a result, the period of Christian beginnings has almost unavoidably been read from hindsight through the lenses of later canon and creed. But if we can remove these lenses, the story of Christian beginnings may sound quite different from the way it has generally been told.

Early Christian communities were characterized by controversy over a wide range of issues. For example, the Letter to the Galatians illustrates how heated debates could become over whether Gentile men who had received salvation in Christ must undergo circumcision, and whether Christian communities should adhere to purity distinctions in their table fellowship. These issues were not battles between true Christians and heretics; instead, they represented early followers of Jesus working out what it means to be a Christian in a world where Jews and Gentiles are sharing meals together. Similarly, the differences among New Testament books are perfectly understandable once we accept that the norm of early Christianity was theological diversity, not consensus. Christian communities had access to a considerable variety of materials and produced diverse versions of Christian thought and practice, using written texts and oral traditions. Churches in different geographical areas had different written texts and oral traditions, so we cannot assume that all churches used or even knew about the same texts.

The Gospel of Mark originally ended at 16:8 with the flight of the astonished women disciples from the empty tomb. The multiformity of early Christianity becomes even more evident when we remove our canonical spectacles. All historians recognize that since the earliest churches lacked a New Testament, limiting the construction of early Christianity to the information given in the New Testament cannot give us the whole story. Historians have to take account of all those materials that are Christian, whether or not they came to reside in the canon, and even if they later were understood to be heretical. Some of the works early Christians possessed, such as the Gospel of the Hebrews or the Gospel of Barnabas, remain lost to us. Others have surfaced among the discoveries from Egypt. These new materials let us see more of the complexity and abundance of early Christian thought.

Despite the theological diversity of early Christianity, one perspective that all the New Testament texts conform to is that the death and resurrection of Jesus and his coming at the end of time are central to salvation. However, this should not lead us to believe that early Christians got their information about the content of Christian teaching and practice from written texts. Most people in the ancient Mediterranean world did not read or write. Instead, people heard about Christianity primarily through preaching and teaching and practiced Christianity through prayer, singing, and table fellowship. While the role of written texts in Christian worship or instruction is unclear, it is clear that the domination of the Bible in our own print culture is an entirely inaccurate model for imagining early Christian life.

Early Christianity was shaped by a complex set of factors, including the controversy over theological issues, diversity in Christian thought and practice, and access to a considerable variety of materials. Despite the challenges of piecing together the history of early Christianity, scholars have made great strides in recent years with the discovery of new materials that let us see more of the complexity and abundance of early Christian thought. By taking into account all those materials that are Christian, whether or not they came to reside in the canon, we can gain a more accurate understanding of the formation of early Christianity and its relevance to our modern world.

The Gospel of Thomas is a collection of sayings of Jesus, lacking any kind of storyline. It does not include accounts of Jesus' birth, death, or resurrection, but does refer to "the living Jesus" as a way of acknowledging his continuing presence. In the Gospel of Thomas, Jesus' teaching takes the focus of salvation, rather than Jesus himself: "Whoever finds the interpretation of these sayings will not experience death." Jesus cautions the disciples not to follow a leader, but to look inside themselves for the kingdom. Jesus is not portrayed as the messiah, Christ, Lord, Son of Man, or Son of God. Saying alludes to his death, but never suggests that his suffering could lead to salvation for others. Rather, Jesus is presented in terms most similar to Jewish Wisdom speculation.

147

In Jewish tradition, Wisdom is described as the co-creator and firstborn of God, as the light, the bringer of life and salvation, as a teacher, and as the designer and controller of history. She comes down to humanity in a variety of guises to offer her wisdom, but is rejected. Similarly, in the Gospel of Thomas, Jesus comes to humanity in the flesh, but finds everyone intoxicated with the world. His teaching gives life; it reveals what is hidden in creation yet beyond human ability to perceive. The Gospel of Thomas is meant to encourage people to seek the kingdom of God within themselves, to uncover the hidden wisdom of God in creation, and to reject worldly pursuits that lead one away from God. Above all, it is Jesus' teaching that leads people to enlightenment and salvation. The Gospel of Truth, written in the second century by theologian Valentinus, interprets Jesus, the Logos or Word of God, as the revelation of God in the world. Jesus was sent to reveal the Father, to be the presence of God in the world. He brings salvation as the teacher of divine knowledge. While the Gospel of Truth acknowledges that Jesus was persecuted and suffered on the cross, it interprets the crucifixion as the publication of his teaching. Jesus was nailed like a public notice upon a wooden pole, the cross. The Gospel of Truth interprets the wooden cross as a type of the Genesis tree of life, and Jesus as the incarnate Word, a kind of book of revelation.

The revelation of Jesus brings about a restoration to unity with the Father by eliminating the deficiencies of ignorance and destroying all the defects of suffering. It brings about authentic existence and awakens people from their nightmare-like state. The Spirit reveals the Son, and the Son's speech brings about the return to the Father, eliminating error and showing the way like a shepherd. The return to the Father does not come about through an apocalyptic catastrophe; rather, it is described as a gentle attraction, a fragrance, and merciful ointment. Souls are said to participate in the Father "by means of kisses." The work states explicitly that it is wrong to think of God as harsh or wrathful; rather, he is without evil, imperturbable, sweet, and all-knowing. The final goal of salvation is rest in the Father. Anyone who is acquainted with the New Testament gospels will find much that seems familiar in these three new gospels, for they all draw from the same pool of early Christian tradition.

Despite the considerable debate and tension among Christians during the first two centuries, early Christian theology and practice were fairly fluid affairs during this period. By the third century, lines hardened as it became increasingly clear that theological views had direct consequences for some very pressing issues. Two new texts dating from the third century, the Apocalypse of Peter and the Testimony of Truth, address some of these issues from perspectives that are new to us.

Understanding the meaning of Jesus on the cross remains an important issue for Christians. Some people agree with the views of these rediscovered texts that the figure of Jesus on the cross contradicts their belief in the goodness of God. However, for many, the image of God suffering on the cross gives meaning and redemptive power to human suffering. The issue is complex, as the symbolism of the cross has been used to justify various forms of abuse, including anti-Judaism. It has sustained suffering rather than empowering people to fight against injustice. Elisabeth Schüssler Fiorenza, a Catholic liberation theologian, argues that the redemptive power of the cross should lead people to solidarity with the poor and the suffering and give hope for resurrection. The debate over the meaning of Jesus on the cross goes to the heart of these vital issues. Examining these controversies helps to understand the meaning of Christian teachings more fully. To fully comprehend the meaning of these new materials, it is essential to read them in their own right. The later Christian tradition is so powerful that it is difficult to avoid automatically placing these new materials into the old structure of the master story. This includes assuming the normative status of the later canon and creed and reading these new materials as deviant. The perspective of the master story is ingrained not only in Christian theology but also in the imagination of historians. It is challenging to imagine that early Christians did not have a New Testament or that Jesus did not establish and authorize the religion of the Nicene Creed.

The standards of orthodoxy and heresy, the appeal to Christian origins for authorization, and the normative status of canon and creed continue to influence scholars. The new works from the Egyptian desert are proving to be very helpful.

149

Mary Magdalene's Works

Mary Magdalene emerged as one of Jesus' key disciples after he exorcised her. She acquired a deep understanding of Jesus' exorcism techniques and became an authority in dealing with unclean spirits. This was due to Jesus' bold claim, "If I throw out demons by God's Spirit, then the kingdom of God has arrived upon you!" However, the Gospels fail to acknowledge Mary's role as a teacher who related Jesus' exorcisms and their significance.

Scholars have identified sources within the Gospels attributed to prominent disciples like Peter. For example, Peter heads the list of the three premier apostles present at the Transfiguration, where they saw their rabbi transformed with heavenly light and speaking with Moses and Elijah (Mark 9:2-8). Evidently, Peter was the principal source of this story, the teacher within Jesus' movement who passed it on and shaped its meaning within Christianity's oral tradition until it made its way to the written Gospels.

The authors of the Gospels are not identified, with each book simply called "According to Mark," "According to Matthew," "According to Luke," and "According to John." The texts themselves infer how the Gospels were produced, by whom, and in what communities of early Christians. Despite the uncertainties involved, thoughtful readers from the start of the second century onward have recognized that the Gospels are not simply books written by individual authors working in isolation. Rather, they are composite editions of different sources that different communities put together in the generations after Jesus' death.

The Gospels emerged a generation after Jesus' death in the major centers of Christianity. Although certainty eludes any attempt to specify when and where the Gospels were composed, a consensus of scholars agrees that Mark was produced in Rome around 73 C.E.; Matthew in Damascus around 80 C.E.; Luke in Antioch on the Orontes around 90 C.E.; and John in Ephesus around 100 C.E. Identifying and analyzing the Gospel sources is vital to get at the best evidence about Jesus and to understand how the Gospels developed as literature.

Peter provided one of these crucial sources. He and his circle of followers prepared people for baptism by reciting an oral narrative of what God had accomplished with Jesus. Preparing would-be converts to Christianity involved a complex and potentially dangerous process in the Greco-Roman world, unlike the routine baptism of infants in much contemporary practice. The worship of Jesus was barely tolerated during the first century, and sometimes civic-minded enthusiasm burst out against the strange new Christian "superstition" (as the Romans categorized Jesus' movement) in the form of violent local pogroms. Because Christianity was perceived as a strange form of Judaism, Christians could also be swept up in outbursts of violence against Jews. A person who claimed to want to be baptized in Jesus' name might, in fact, be an informer for the magistrate of a city or, worse still, for a gang of narrow-minded thugs.

Peter was especially involved with preparing converts for baptism, and it makes good sense to see him as the source of passages in the Gospels that name him explicitly or that directly concern his baptismal agenda. When scholars tie together a disciple's name with the ritual agenda of that disciple and the oral source he developed, they establish what amounts to that disciple's signature within the source. In the case of Peter, he is named repeatedly within passages that were crucial to preparing converts for baptism, so it is widely agreed he had a profound influence on the formation of the Gospels.

If we apply the same logic and refer to the same kind of evidence that has been applied to Peter, Mary Magdalene also emerges as the author of a source of stories that bear her oral signature. She was the single most important conduit of stories concerning Jesus' exorcisms.

The first exorcism story, set in the Capernaum synagogue, depicts unclean spirits whose threat dissolves once they are confronted with purity. This account clearly reveals Mary Magdalene's oral signature. Her perspective governs the presentation of the story, reflecting an insider's knowledge of the deep inner struggle that exorcism involved for a person who was possessed.

151

Capernaum was a wealthy enough town that its Jewish population could afford to build an actual structure for its "synagogue," a designation that referred in the first century to a congregation of Israelites, with or without a building. This first public act of Jesus in the Gospel According to Mark therefore unfolds in a comparatively dignified space, a small building fitted with benches, where the assembly could comfortably settle local disputes, hear and discuss Scripture, delegate the priestly duties that local Levites fulfilled in Jerusalem, arrange for the collection and transfer of taxes to the Temple, and participate in rituals such as circumcision and burial.

In Mary's story, any routine is disrupted when an unclean spirit confronts Jesus. The demon "speaks," but the people in the synagogue hear only inarticulate shrieks. Jesus alone understands the meaning of the sounds. The demon identifies itself with all unclean demons of the spirit world in a fascinating switch of pronouns in the text "We have nothing for you, Nazarene Jesus! Have you come to destroy us? I know who you are—the holy one of God!"

Jesus viewed the violence of demons as a sign of their impending defeat. In addition to its identification with unclean spirits as a whole, the demon in the synagogue also specifies the purpose of Jesus' exorcisms: not simple banishment, but their definitive removal from power. That is what the demon fears on behalf of the whole realm of unclean spirits: regime change instigated by Jesus as the agent of God's Kingdom, the kind of demonic retreat Mary Magdalene had experienced.

Fearing destruction, the unclean spirits act before Jesus speaks, initiating a preemptive strike by naming him. Mary's source describes this as a very noisy event. The demon "cried out". Jesus shouted back in the rough language of the street, "Shut up, and get out from him!" The demon's obedience came under protest; it "convulsed" its nameless victim and departed with a scream.

These astute observations all point toward a storyteller with profound knowledge of the intense struggle with evil that Jesus' exorcisms entailed, their uproarious quality, and the peril that the exorcist would be defeated. Furthermore, the storyteller knew how Jesus interpreted the demons' wordless shout, as an admission of ultimate defeat. Whoever conveyed this story had to have known both what went on and what Jesus thought about it. Mary Magdalene best fits the description of that storyteller.

By considering Mary's influence, it becomes clear why Mark's accounts of exorcism differ from most ancient stories. Instead of portraying Jesus as a self-assured exorcist, Mark's narratives depict the demons as violently resisting him. This is particularly evident in the second story from the Magdalene source, which takes place in Decapolis, just across the Sea of Galilee from Magdala.

It was unusual in the ancient world to insist that the demons formed a violent, coordinated front of impurity, and bizarre to depict them as dictating how an exorcist should handle them. The legion story deliberately engages in exaggeration, to the point that no commentator has been able to draw the line between the story's symbolic meaning and the literal event it depicts. Still, the symbolic meaning remains clear no matter how literally we take the details: As the divine Kingdom takes root, Rome will be dislodged. Roman demons are no more threatening than panicked pigs; they will neutralize themselves in God's encompassing purity, which is as deep as the sea. Definitive exorcism signaled an ultimate change in humanity within Jesus' vision and in Mary's experience. In her narrative, the man who had been possessed with a legion of demons went on to become the first messenger of Jesus in Gentile territory. After his return from Decapolis to Galilee, Jesus sent out twelve of his disciples. They acted on his behalf, announcing the Kingdom, healing people, cleansing them of impurity, throwing out their demons. When they did so, Jesus said that he saw Satan fall like lightning from heaven, robbed of his old power. Removing impurity by naming it made Satan fall, and other teachings of Jesus unconnected with the stories Mary told confirm this perspective.

The Gospels insist on the violence of the confrontation between Jesus and unclean spirits precisely because it demonstrates the cosmic significance of his actions. As Jesus pressed home the significance of removing demons from people, he evolved as a religious persona. He became increasingly prophetic —his words and deeds took on the character of signs, indicating how God was acting or about to act in the world. Jesus and Mary Magdalene explained why demons shouted at Jesus, and he back at them: They resisted him, crying out his name and spiritual identity, because their encounter with him was a war of worlds. Mary told the story of the legion of demons from the sympathetic perspective of someone who could speak from firsthand experience of being exorcised. A legion consisted of some six thousand soldiers, and auxiliary troops co-opted by the legion could equal that number.

Although Mary's seven demons were by no means literally legion, she could tell this story because she knew the real depth of the cosmic antagonism involved in Jesus' exorcism and had felt that antagonism in her own body. Immediately before the third principal exorcism story in the Magdalene source, Jesus—transformed in divine glory and talking with Moses and Elijah—appears to Peter, James, and John. Just as he manifested himself to his disciples in the visionary experience of the Transfiguration as a master comparable to Elijah and Moses, so the story in Mary's source expresses Jesus' vehement insistence on the power of Spirit in contrast to the tentative quality of the efforts of his disciples, who had been unable to deal with the demon at hand. Jesus explained to them: "This sort can go out by nothing except by prayer."

By this time, he was heading toward his final days in Jerusalem, and Jesus had become a master exorcist, locked in cosmic struggle with Satan in a way that was beyond his followers' capacity to emulate and sometimes even to understand. As his own spirituality evolved, Jesus had found ways to magnify awareness that all impurity dissolves in the holiness of Spirit, and Mary Magdalene was there to trace that development. She knew Jesus' method in this domain inside and out, and exorcism stories from her source reflect this knowledge.

In the first story, set in Capernaum's synagogue, the demon defeated itself by acknowledging the purity it confronted in Jesus, "the holy one of God," and Jesus' technique could involve—as in the case of the "legion"—giving unclean spirits what they said they wanted to speed their departure.

Listening to Mary Magdalene's source can help us understand not only Mary, but also a charismatic and prophetic strand of Christianity rooted in Jesus' practice. This impulse, adamantly confronts the forces of uncleanness with the power of God's Spirit.

While not all of Jesus' followers embraced the violence of his exorcisms all the time, we learn of this from another run of material that spells out Jesus' exorcistic theory in his own words and represents his conflict with those around him. This teaching confirms, from Jesus' point of view, exactly the sense of cosmic struggle and resistance that the Magdalene source narrates.

Mark's Gospel indicates that once Jesus' family tried to seize him physically, thinking him to be "beside himself." If you did not share Jesus' vision, he could easily seem to be out of his mind. Rabbis of this period also characterized another mystic, Simon ben Zoma, as "beside himself" because he was prone to ecstasy in the midst of daily life.

Jesus' family's conventional concern only stoked his insistence on confrontation with Satan. He battled directly in his exorcisms with "the strong man," the honcho of all demons. Rabbi Jesus said, "No one, however, can enter the home of the strong man to rob his vessels unless he first binds the strong man, and then he will rob his home." Once he was bound, Jesus could pillage his goods! Jesus didn't want to leave a possessed person's body open for unclean spirits to return to with ever more impure companions; instead, he would sweep Satan out of house and home.

He was convinced that Satan's defeat completed the Kingdom's arrival; one implied the other, and the Spirit of God effected them both. When the Spirit—conceived of as female in Jesus' theology—moves in this world, she displaces demons and installs divine justice.

Jesus said that denying the Holy Spirit was the one sin that would not be pardoned. "Everything will be forgiven people, sins and curses (as much as they curse), but whoever curses the Holy Spirit will never ever have release but is liable for a perpetual sin." The unpardonable sin is to deny the Holy Spirit as she transforms the world by dissolving evil. The consistency of Jesus' thinking about exorcism is striking, and echoes the Magdalene source.

Luke's naming of Mary in personal connection with repeated exorcisms enables us to say that Mary Magdalene told stories about Jesus—especially the detailed stories of his exorcisms—that we can read today in the Gospels. She then takes her place beside apostles who also influenced how the message about Jesus was preached and taught. The exorcism stories in the Gospels bear her signature. One of the most vital and enduring teachings of Jesus she helped craft concerned how the power from God could dissolve evil by letting it name itself for what it was. She showed how he put that teaching into practice. Medieval legend conveyed its awareness of Mary's importance within this field in its own way. Gherardesca da Pisa, who died in 1269, spoke of Mary as intervening in her own bloody battle with a demon, then as helping her care for her wounds.

Mary knew that the demons' most fearsome weapon, deployed to resist Jesus' exorcism, was their unique knowledge of his identity. Up until the point of the first exorcism story in Mark, no one in the Gospel had called Jesus "the holy one of God." No one would ever call him that again. The demons expressed insight into Jesus' mysterious identity, what scholars for more than a century have called "the messianic secret." By telling this story and stories like it, Mary indicated that she knew this secret. The nameless man in Capernaum's synagogue alone named Jesus as "the holy one of God"; the man with the legion of demons uniquely called Jesus "Son of highest God" (Mark 5:7). Mary Magdalene, Jesus' companion in exorcism, understood the secret that his struggle with the demons involved.

The unclean spirit in the synagogue designated Jesus as a source of purity, "the holy one of God." That is why Jesus' presence was a threat to that demon and the demonic world as a whole. The unspecified number of demons in the synagogue, the "legion" in the cemetery, the demon who resisted Jesus' disciples, the "seven" who departed from Mary Magdalene— all in their different ways signal the demonic axis as a whole. The spiritual combat between Jesus and the forces of impurity was resolved because the unclean spirits recognized purity when they experienced it. Violent though their rebellion seemed, the demons ultimately recognized their own nonexistence. Their only power was denial. They could rebel against God's pure purpose, but only with the empty complaint of their own impotence. Finally, the demons had no power at all. They drowned in their own knowledge as surely as the legion did once they revealed themselves in the pigs. In Mary's telling, Rome itself headed toward the same fate.

The Gospels present only three detailed stories of the exorcisms of Jesus. In each of them, the emphasis on Jesus' assertion of the purity of Spirit, the resistance of the demonic world, impurity, struggle, and the possessed person's breakthrough to integrity come to vivid, precise expression. This oral source, which shines through the tightly coordinated but different versions in Matthew, Mark, and Luke, is the nearest approach there is to Jesus' actual technique of meeting the challenge of uncleanness and evil. Not only in cases of exorcism, which have a long history in the West, but also in Christian approaches to the miseries of addiction, compulsion, aimless violence, and purposeful wrongdoing by people and nations, the basic faith that evil named is evil removed has animated the conduct of millions of people who have read the Gospels. Mary Magdalene, anonymously but effectively, has instructed them all.

Mary Magdalene and Jesus's Movement

Mary Magdalene played a crucial role in the life and teachings of Rabbi Jesus. She emerged as the most influential woman in Jesus' movement due to her actions, teachings, and character. She was also his steadfast partner during the most difficult period of his life. This period began when Jesus was forced to flee from Capernaum under the threat of death from Herod Antipas. He spent four years wandering and experimenting with forays into Gentile territory east and west of Galilee, but his hostility to Gentile living proved incompatible with sustained residence among non-Israelites.

Mary must have traveled with Jesus during this period, witnessing his exorcisms, including the one in Decapolis. However, her travel was limited by her vulnerability as a woman, which was a significant disadvantage during that time. Jesus coordinated his movements with his other disciples, who lived in the towns and villages of Galilee, healing in the way Jesus had taught them, casting out demons, announcing the Kingdom of God, and praying and sharing meals together. Mary was part of this group, and her role extended beyond being a skilled practitioner of exorcism. She was also an adept of other spiritual practices, including anointing, which was associated with exorcism and healing.

Mary Magdalene and other women "served" or "ministered to" Jesus and his disciples, which included financial support, lodging, work with one's hands, and labor for the divine Kingdom. Mary's anointing was a form of provision at least as valuable as money. Jesus recognized that the Spirit was the engine of his action and teaching, the driving force of his exorcisms in particular. He wanted his followers to anoint people, as anointing conveyed Spirit. Mary Magdalene and her companions took up this programmatic activity, as did the more famous apostles.

The Gospel According to Luke ignores Mary Magdalene's anointing of Jesus prior to his death, which is a significant omission. Nonetheless, the story helpfully illustrates that women other than Mary Magdalene practiced anointing within Jesus' movement. Mary's anointing was a vital part of Jesus' teachings and practices, and she was its preeminent practitioner.

It is noteworthy that Jesus' teachings and practices were not limited to exorcism and anointing. He coordinated his movements with his disciples, who lived in the towns and villages of Galilee, healing in the way Jesus had taught them, casting out demons, announcing the Kingdom of God, and meditating on the presence of God's Spirit in their midst as they prayed and shared meals together. Mary was part of this group, and her role extended beyond being a skilled practitioner of exorcism. She was also an adept of other spiritual practices.

Mary Magdalene was much more than a skilled practitioner of exorcism. She was also an active participant in the pilgrimage that Jesus led to Jerusalem for the Feast of Tabernacles, where he believed he and his followers could change the world and welcome God's Kingdom into the land of Israel by offering sacrifice on Mount Zion in the way that the God of Israel desired. Following the prophecy of Zechariah, Rabbi Jesus believed that true sacrifice would bring both the end of Israel's oppression and the opening of the Temple to all humanity, both Jews and non-Jews. Mary Magdalene was with him when Jesus arrived in Jerusalem, galvanizing the festal crowds during the feast of Sukkot (or Tabernacles) in the autumn of 31 C.E. During this tumultuous period, Mary witnessed Jesus' reaction when he learned that Caiaphas, the high priest of the time, had authorized trading in the Temple, instead of maintaining the ancient practice—and Zechariah's prophecy—that Israelites offer the work of their own hands there. She observed the planning in Bethany for Jesus' onslaught on the Temple, when a small army of disciples and enthusiasts, some 150 or 200 men, joined Jesus one morning to drive out the vendors and the animals Caiaphas had allowed in the Temple's twenty-five-acre southern outer court.

She was also aware of Jesus' reaction when he discovered that one of his sympathizers in Jerusalem, a thug named Barabbas, had committed murder during the Temple raid.

MARY AT JESUS RESURRECTION AND TRANSFIGURATION

Jesus' Resurrection occurred before anyone could grasp its significance: That is the unequivocal message of Mark, the earliest Gospel, in its original form. The Gospel's climax presents a visionary experience, which Mark evokes with its spare poetry. Three women, led by Mary Magdalene, saw a vision and heard angelic words. Mark conveys their bewilderment in the face of revelation (16:1-8): And when Sabbath elapsed, Mary the Magdalene and Mary of James and Salome purchased spices so they could go anoint him. And very early on the first of the Sabbaths they came upon the tomb when the sun dawned. And they were saying to one another, Who will roll the stone away from the opening of the tomb for us? They looked up and perceived that the stone had been rolled off (because it was exceedingly big). They went towards the tomb and saw a young man sitting on the right appareled in a white robe, and they were completely astonished.

But he says to them: "Do not be completely astonished. You see't Jesus the crucified Nazarene. He is raised; he is not here. Look—the place where they laid him. But depart, tell his students and Peter that he goes before you into Galilee; you will see him there, just as he said to you". They went out and fled from the tomb, because trembling and frenzy had them. And they said nothing to any one; they were afraid, because— This abrupt ending climaxes the primitive but effective art of Mark, signaling how hard and disruptive it was, even for those intimate with Jesus, to grapple with the vision that signaled he had overcome death. From a prosaic point of view, this truncated finale makes the Gospel seem defective. How could anyone end a story by saying "they were afraid, because—"? In later manuscripts of Mark, this apparent gap was dutifully filled in with now-familiar stories culled from the other Gospels of the risen Jesus appearing to his disciples. Pious scribes frequently harmonized the texts of the Gospels, making them look alike. These additions are transparent, and Mark's stark, primitive ending, the apogee of its art of revelation, stands out because of its powerful originality.

In the Gospel's original form, the three women are the first to know that Jesus had been raised from the dead. Mark names Mary Magdalene first in this account and her cognomen, "the Magdalene," resonates, as I mentioned in chapter 2, with Jesus"—"the Nazarene." Mary is on her way with Mary of James and Salome to anoint Jesus' corpse, and that reinforces the point made in chapter 5—that the Magdalene had been the nameless anointer who prepared Jesus before his death for burial. Mary's every action and response are crucial to an understanding of her realization that God had raised Jesus from the dead. It was customary, as well as a commandment of the Torah, that Israelites attend to the corpses of relatives and friends, even victims of crucifixion. A first-century ossuary, discovered outside Jerusalem in 1968, contains the bones of a young man named Yochanan. An iron spike with an attached piece of wood is embedded in his right heel. Properly tending to the dead was incumbent on every Israelite, and any Roman official would court rebellion by deliberately flouting that imperative. The Jerusalem prefect must have released Yochanan's broken body for burial; his ossuary indicates that the Romans honored Israelite tradition.

Following ancient practice, those who received Yochanan's crucified corpse bathed and anointed it, wrapping the body in linen and placing it in a funerary cave. According to usual burial practice, they deposited the bones in a limestone box after a year and carved Yochanan's name on the ossuary's side. This discovery directly contradicts the claim, fashionable for more than a century, that Jesus' body was tossed to the dogs after his execution. Foundational texts of Judaism give precise instructions for dealing with corpses after crucifixion; a dead body that was exposed was a source of impurity and offended God. Mary and her companions returned to Jesus' tomb in order to fulfill the Torah's commandment, having waited until sundown on the Sabbath so that they could buy materials for anointing Jesus' corpse. Modern readers often express disgust and incredulity at the thought of returning to a corpse that had already been interred for some thirty-six hours. But mourners in antiquity were not squeamish: Death had not yet been banished to the mortician's ghetto and anointing featured importantly in customs of burial in the ancient Near East.

Death's impurity had to be dealt with, and people accepted the temporary uncleanness of handling the corpse in order to ensure the purity of the land and the community of Israel.

The Talmud describes not only practices of cleaning, anointing, and wrapping the dead but also the custom of visiting the tomb each day for three days after a burial to make certain that the deceased was truly dead, not simply unconscious. The Talmud in question is the Babylonian Talmud (also called the Bavli), which is later than the Talmud of Jerusalem but nonetheless constitutes the pivotal text of Rabbinic Judaism. The story of the resuscitation of Lazarus in John 11:1-44 presupposes that custom. The Talmud speaks of people going on to lead healthy lives, as Lazarus did, when dedicated relatives and friends discovered they had, in fact, been interred alive. The moment of natural death can seem strangely uncertain, as anyone who has visited the terminally ill and their families knows. A woman once asked me to come to her home, unsure of whether cancer had at last claimed her husband's life. That kind of doubt is natural; the recovery of the supposedly dead sometimes defies medical technology. I gave the man last rites but stayed with his family until a medical practitioner could confirm his death.

Until then, the family lived through the same limbo that ancient Jewish mourners endured for three days—more in the case of Lazarus. This concern—to be sure a living person is not treated as dead—stems from a deep regard for life. In the ancient Israelite ethos, caring for a person extended to taking care of his body until the transition from life to death was complete. Crucifixion at the hands of the Romans left virtually no room for uncertainty over the fact of death and required the treatment of a badly damaged corpse. Puncture wounds leaked blood and lymphatic fluid, and bits of broken bone extruded; victims who had been flogged prior to crucifixion were covered with deep gashes. In Jesus' case, a javelin had also been thrust into his body.

The Roman Empire was in the business of death, using crucifixion as the supreme punishment to terrorize recalcitrant subjects in its dominions between Spain and Syria. They had learned this technique of state terror from the Persian Empire, then went on to master and monopolize it.

Crucifixion was a punishment that only the Roman authorities themselves— rather than their client kings or other petty rulers—could inflict. These executioners knew what they were doing, and theories that Jesus somehow physically survived the cross represent a combination of fantasy, revisionism, and half-baked science. The women did not go to the tomb to confirm that Jesus was dead, but to anoint and care for what they knew all too well was a corpse. The women had joined Joseph of Arimathea, a sympathetic rabbi who offered his own family's burial cave to be used for Jesus' interment (Mark 15:42-46). But the observance of the Sabbath (which arrived at sunset) prevented them from purchasing or preparing anointment at the time Jesus was buried. Their delay was therefore natural, calibrated to the rhythm of observant Judaism. To complete the dutiful care of their dead rabbi, Mary and the women made their way to the tomb. Perfumed oil for rubbing on the dead was scented with the resin of myrrh and the leaves of aloe . The astringent properties of the aloe helped to seal skin made porous by death. The smell of myrrh was associated in the mind of any dedicated Israelite with the aroma of the Temple. Both these scents were also used in the luxurious perfume that a lover might enjoy on the body of the beloved. Suspensions of myrrh and aloe were delicate mixtures, produced by seething them in oil and aging the unction in stone containers.

In the case of Jesus, a rabbi named Nicodemus saw to the expense so that Mary Magdalene and her companions could purchase the salve from a sympathetic vendor in Jerusalem, who was willing to make the sale as soon as the setting sun brought an end to the Sabbath. They bought their oil and spices so that they "could go anoint" the body of Jesus. To say they had to "go" for that purpose suggests they walked a distance; one ancient manuscript of the New Testament says they "proceeded", implying an even longer journey.

This choice of words embarrassed later copyists, who eliminated any reference to the women's travel because it contradicted the tradition that Jesus was buried in the Church of the Holy Sepulcher, one of Christianity's greatest pilgrimage (and hence tourist) sites since the fourth century. Modern archaeology has discredited the notion that this church is the site of Jesus' grave.

Mary Magdalene and her companions found Jesus' tomb in a recognized cemetery well outside the city—a place where prominent people, such as Joseph of Arimathea, purchased caves for family burial. The archaeological evidence for the existence of such sites is now secure. In 1990, on a hill dotted with natural caves in the Arab hamlet of Abu Tor, a mile and a half south of the Temple, the ossuary of Caiaphas, the high priest at the time of Jesus' execution, was discovered. There is little doubt whose ossuary this is: The limestone box was found in situ, with Caiaphas's name written on it twice. A coin discovered in the same cave bears the imprint of Herod Agrippa I, which shows that burial took place in the mid-forties of the first century. The carving on the box picks up the symbolism of the Temple, signaling Caiaphas's status as high priest. Was it in this cemetery that Joseph of Arimathea, a member of the same council to which the high priest belonged, interred the corpse of Jesus? Certainty escapes us, but it is clear that the women as described in Mark went to a private and remote place, much more like Abu Tor than the site of the Church of the Holy Sepulcher inside the city. Taking place well outside the city, far from earshot or the prying eyes of opponents, the experience at the mouth of the tomb was the women's alone.

The three women met there privately with Jesus, just as three men—Peter, James, and John—did on the mountain of the Transfiguration. In the experience of both female and male disciples, revelation came as a communal vision that intensified each individual's insight. Vision crystallized the women's conviction that Jesus was alive, a vibrant spiritual presence despite his shameful death. It was their Transfiguration.

165

Ancient Judaism conceived of visionary reality as an experience that could be shared—and it was this Transfiguration at the mouth of the tomb that emerged as the force that ultimately turned Jesus' movement into a new religion.

The Transfiguration and Jesus' Resurrection provoked astonishment and awe, highlighting the mystical qualities of encounters with the divine in Mark's Gospel. When Jesus performed an exorcism in the Capernaum synagogue, Mark describes the people there as "all were astonished." This scene establishes a clear pattern in the Gospel: astonishment and awe were a litmus test of revelation. The peasants of Galilee yearned for transformation into the Kingdom of God, which some rabbis of the time called ha-olam haba, or "the age to come," when the power of God's eternal Throne would transcend all divisions, heal all ills, and overpower the petty tyrannies of a broken world. Any experience or sign that offered a glimpse into this ultimate reality provoked awestruck joy.

Visionary prophets such as Ezekiel and mystical practitioners of Judaism after him conceived of this divine power as "the Chariot." The divine Chariot was nothing other than the Throne of God, which Moses and his companions (Aaron, Nadab, Abihu, and seventy elders of Israel) saw in its sapphire glory. Like the Resurrection of Jesus, the Chariot was open to communal vision and could unveil itself anywhere, anytime. Jewish texts from before, during, and after the first century show that rabbis practiced the unveiling of the Chariot in this world by means of disciplined meditation. Visions were not just spontaneous experiences that burst in on passive recipients; adepts could realize the Chariot through their dedicated practice.

Rabbi Jesus trained his disciples, including Mary Magdalene, in the tradition of the Merkavah, the Chariot, from the time she met him in Galilee through the period of his final pilgrimage to Jerusalem.

They attuned themselves to the divine Chariot, helped by Scriptures they memorized, disciplines they handed on by word of mouth, and examples of their master's teaching and practice that they emulated. Astonishment in God's presence became their way of life.

This astonishment strikes Peter, James, and John during the Transfiguration, when Jesus is transformed before them into a gleaming white figure. They see him speaking with Moses and Elijah, the two most powerful prophets of Israel's Scriptures. Jesus' visions began as his own personal revelations, but years of communal meditation made his experiences transparent to his disciples. On the mountain of his Transfiguration, Jesus followed in the footsteps of Moses, who took three of his followers (Aaron, Nadab, and Abihu) up Mount Sinai (Exodus 24:1-11), where they sacrificed and banqueted to celebrate their vision of the God of Israel on his sapphire Throne.

But unlike what happened on Sinai, Jesus' disciples, covered by a shining cloud of glory, also heard a voice: "This is my Son, the beloved, in whom I take pleasure: hear him." When the cloud passed, Moses and Elijah had disappeared. Jesus stood alone as God's Son. Divine "Son" was the designation that Jesus had heard when, as an adolescent, encamped on the River Jordan with his rabbi, John the Baptist, he had practiced mystical ascension; now his own disciples saw and heard the truth of his personal vision. Jesus' true genius lay in the transparency of his visionary experience.

When Jesus was immersed in the Spirit, the voice that came from heaven did not speak in the exclusive language of the later doctrine of the Trinity, which made Jesus into the only (and only possible) "Son of God." Rather, Jesus' immersion in Spirit enabled him to initiate others into that experience. Likewise, the voice from the luminous cloud in the Transfiguration signaled that the divine Spirit, which had animated Moses and Elijah, was present in Jesus and that Jesus could pass on that Spirit to his followers, each of whom could also become a child, or "Son," of God.

The whole Gospel According to Mark is designed as a program to train its hearers and readers for the moment of baptism, when they, too, will experience the Spirit within them and call upon God as their Abba, their father and true source.

Jesus knew that everyone's perceptions, including his own, had to change and adjust to this transcendent vision. As God's own Son, he was as confused as every Son who would ever follow the path he marked, taking up a cross and crossing over into the world of glory. This pattern of confusion in the face of revelation climaxes in Jesus' Resurrection. This experience manifested what theologians often refer to as the "presence" of God in this world, although the word "presence" scarcely conveys the inexhaustible dynamism of the Chariot, which welded human consciousness to God's as he founded the universe, maintained its precarious existence moment by moment, and was poised to sweep it all away at will.

Christianity became highly philosophical and often abstract from the second century onward, but Jesus and his Judaic contemporaries did not share the abstractions that have become common currency in the language of the divine world. For Rabbi Jesus, the word God conveyed not a philosophical idea but the ultimate reality—beautiful and fearsome and overpowering. At the mouth of the tomb, Mary Magdalene and her companions were taught definitively by Jesus that God was the only, ultimate truth—the omnipotent, swirling vortex of creation.

Although the Transfiguration itself and the vision of the women at the mouth of the tomb obviously reflect different experiences, both revealed Jesus' divine identity and thoroughly unnerved his disciples. Fear silenced the apostles on Mount Hebron, as though they were caught in a dream, unable to speak. Their silence prefigures the silence of the three women at the mouth of the tomb. In these cases, the disciples' astonishment signals a vision of the heavenly court, where the Chariot Throne of God is clouded in awe and radiates divine power.

Mark indicates that the women left our world and fearfully entered this realm. Both the Transfiguration and Mary's vision intimately connect Jesus to the Throne of God. In the Transfiguration, he appears in an altered form, shining in brilliance with Moses and Elijah, prophets who, it was understood in the first century, had "not tasted death," a turn of phrase shared among Jewish, Christian, and Gnostic texts. The phrase does not refer to escaping physical death, but to transcending its consequences. Vision gave access to a world where death no longer had dominion. Instead, dying marked an entry into God's presence.

The role of Mary Magdalene in the resurrection story is a topic of great significance in the study of the Gospels. The differences in how her story is presented in each of the four Gospels (Matthew, Mark, Luke, and John) reveal not only the unique styles and poetics of each Gospel but also provide insight into the early Christian communities who produced them.

The Gospel of Matthew, for instance, shows a break in the link between Mary's ritual anointing and Jesus' Resurrection. This attenuates her role, but an even deeper reduction in her importance, as compared to Mark, follows. Matthew undermines the women's vision at the tomb. Before describing Mary's experience with her colleagues, Matthew alludes to an earthquake that symbolizes Jesus' triumph over death. This legendary event appears only in Matthew's Gospel and has no historical source from the period. The scene in Matthew is no longer purely visionary, as it is in Mark, but a supernatural intervention into the physical world with tangible consequences. The women are completely passive, as if they were "as dead," like the guards.

Despite the differences, each Gospel is unique and develops a poetics all its own. Matthew was composed in Damascus, over a thousand miles away from Mark's Rome, in a city that Israel's prophets had long associated with the power of God's Spirit. In the years before there was any formal division between Judaism and Christianity, Jesus' followers saw their master as the fulfillment of Israel's destiny, and most of them worked out their peculiar vision in peace with their Jewish neighbors.

By the time Matthew's Gospel was written around 80 C.E., the leaders of churches in Damascus clearly saw themselves as separate from the synagogues there, and they stopped using the designation "rabbi" altogether. But Matthew also shows that the importance of vision had in no way diminished. This Gospel speaks of Jesus coming back to earth with his angels to judge all the nations, dividing them up into sheep and goats according to how people had behaved toward one another during their lives. Matthew's poetics pivot on the impact of apocalypse on the material world, just as Mark's poetics pivot on the silent amazement that revelation brings.

Despite sidelining Mary Magdalene's vision, Matthew does not completely erase her, any more than Mark did. This incomplete erasure underscores her pivotal role as the prime herald of Jesus' Resurrection. Matthew even admits what Mark only implies: after her angelic vision, Mary actually encounters the risen Jesus. Matthew's women not only see the angel, but they also meet Jesus himself as they depart from the mouth of the tomb. Matthew spells out what Mark implies—that the story of the women at the mouth of the tomb points toward a later encounter with Jesus himself.

The importance of physical reality in Luke's Gospel is even more pronounced. Luke has Mary and her companions search the tomb and find it empty. Likewise, Luke has the risen Jesus insist on his own physical reality. Only in this Gospel does Jesus explicitly say, "See my hands and my feet, that I am myself. Feel me and see, because a spirit does not have flesh and bone just as you perceive I have." Jesus even eats some fish to prove that his Resurrection is substantial and material. Despite this, in Luke's Gospel, Mary's vision becomes a brutal suppression. Mary Magdalene's whole orientation subverted Luke's materialism, and the women's testimony is dismissed as "nonsense" by the male disciples.

For Luke's Gospel, only Jesus personally, raised from the dead in flesh and bone, can explain his resurrected presence among his disciples.

The Gospel of John presents Mary Magdalene as the first person to witness the Resurrection. She is shown to be a central figure who has a significant role in the early Christian community. John's Gospel presents Mary as a figure of great faith and devotion to Jesus, who is rewarded with a vision of the risen Christ. In John's Gospel, Mary is the first person to see Jesus after his Resurrection, and she is the one who announces the good news to the disciples. Luke's Gospel indirectly references Mary's understanding of Jesus' practice of exorcism (8:2), as previously mentioned. However, this does not make the Gospel feminist because mentioning women is not the same as including them as active agents in Jesus' ministry and Resurrection. Luke utilized sources that apparently conveyed women's perspectives, but the Gospel itself maintains a different viewpoint that focuses on the unique authority of male apostles in Jerusalem.

When Luke presents a woman named Mary as choosing "the good part" of being a disciple by sitting at Jesus' feet instead of serving him, the Gospel takes care to clarify that this is Mary, Martha's sister, not Mary Magdalene. This ensures that the woman is not associated with any tradition or source that could rival the apostolic authority in Jerusalem. She doesn't even speak. Nevertheless, Jesus' mother, who is addressed by the angel Gabriel, identifies herself as "the slave of the Lord". Luke's dedication to the hierarchy of the Jerusalem apostles, combined with a view of the Resurrection that is, in its own way, as materialistic as Matthew's, resulted in the marginalization of the Magdalene, her vision, her source, and her practice of anointing.

In conclusion, the different portrayals of Mary Magdalene's role in the Resurrection story in the four Gospels reflect the unique styles and poetics of each Gospel and provide insight into the communities that produced them. While there are differences in the portrayal of Mary Magdalene, her importance as a witness to the Resurrection remains consistent throughout the Gospels.

The Apocryphal and Gnostic Gospel of Judas

Introduction: The Lost Gospel

In the vast sands of Egypt, during the 1970s, a remarkable discovery was made that would send ripples through the world of biblical scholarship and theology. Hidden away for centuries, a manuscript emerged that bore the name of one of the most controversial figures in Christian history: Judas Iscariot. This was the Gospel of Judas.

The discovery of the Gospel of Judas was not just an archaeological triumph; it was a theological enigma. For centuries, Judas had been vilified as the betrayer, the disciple who handed Jesus over to the authorities for thirty pieces of silver. Yet, this gospel painted a radically different picture. Here, Judas was not the traitor but a chosen confidant, privy to secret teachings and cosmic truths that Jesus shared with no other. The implications of this portrayal were profound. It challenged long-held beliefs about Judas's role in the Passion narrative and raised questions about the very nature of betrayal and divine purpose.

But the Gospel of Judas did not exist in isolation. It was a part of a broader tapestry of early Christian writings, many of which never made it into the canonical Bible. These texts, often labeled as "apocryphal" or "Gnostic," offer a window into the diverse and vibrant world of early Christianity. A world where different communities, each with their own interpretations of Jesus's teachings, vied for legitimacy and recognition.

The term "apocryphal" refers to writings that, for various reasons, were not included in the official canon of Scripture. Some were deemed heretical, while others simply fell out of favor or were overshadowed by more popular texts. Yet, they provide invaluable insights into the beliefs, debates, and struggles of early Christian communities. Gnosticism, on the other hand, was a movement that emphasized personal spiritual knowledge over orthodox teachings and rituals.

Gnostic texts, like the Gospel of Judas, often contain esoteric teachings and present a more mystical interpretation of Christian doctrine.

They speak of a divine spark within every individual and a cosmic struggle between the forces of light and darkness.

The emergence of the Gospel of Judas from the shadows of history was not without its controversies. Scholars debated its authenticity, theologians pondered its implications, and the public was captivated by its message. But beyond the debates and sensational headlines, the Gospel of Judas invites us to reflect on the complexities of faith, history, and the ever-evolving understanding of sacred truth.

As we delve deeper into this text and its context, we are reminded that history is not always written by the victors. Sometimes, voices from the margins emerge to challenge, enlighten, and inspire. The Gospel of Judas is one such voice, beckoning us to listen, question, and seek.

The World of Gnosticism

In the early centuries of Christianity, as the nascent religion spread across the Mediterranean and encountered a myriad of cultures and philosophies, it birthed a plethora of interpretations and beliefs. Among the most intriguing and enigmatic of these early Christian movements was Gnosticism. The term "Gnostic" is derived from the Greek word "gnosis," meaning "knowledge." But for the Gnostics, this wasn't just any knowledge; it was a profound, mystical understanding that promised liberation from the material world's confines.

The Gnostics viewed the universe as a battleground between opposing forces of light and darkness. They believed that a supreme, unknowable God, far removed from human comprehension, existed beyond this realm of conflict. This divine entity emanated lesser divine beings or "aeons," each representing various aspects of the divine essence. However, a rupture in the divine realm led to the creation of the material world, governed by a lesser deity often referred to as the "demiurge." This demiurge, in Gnostic thought, was ignorant of the supreme God and, in his arrogance, believed himself to be the sole deity. The material world he ruled over was seen as imperfect, a prison for the divine spark present within certain humans.

Humanity's plight, according to Gnostic belief, was the result of being trapped in the physical realm, ensnared by ignorance and forgetfulness of their true divine nature. This is where the role of "gnosis" or secret knowledge came into play. Gnostics thought that salvation wasn't achieved merely through faith or good deeds, but by acquiring this hidden knowledge. This knowledge was not intellectual but experiential, a transformative realization that allowed individuals to reconnect with the divine source and transcend the material world's limitations.

The role of secret knowledge in Gnostic traditions cannot be overstated. Gnostic texts, often written in the form of gospels or revelations, were filled with esoteric teachings, allegories, and myths that aimed to guide initiates on their spiritual journey. These writings were not meant for the uninitiated. They required guidance, often provided by Gnostic teachers or communities, to decipher and internalize.

The Gospel of Thomas, for instance, is a collection of sayings attributed to Jesus that often eschew clear interpretation, beckoning the reader to delve deeper, to seek and find.

But this emphasis on secret knowledge was also a source of contention. To the orthodox Christian establishment, the Gnostics' secretive practices and disdain for the material world were heretical. The idea that salvation could be achieved outside the Church's sacraments and hierarchy was seen as a direct challenge to its authority. As a result, Gnostic teachings were often suppressed, their texts destroyed, and their communities marginalized.

Yet, the allure of Gnosticism, with its promise of hidden truths and spiritual liberation, persisted. Even today, the echoes of Gnostic thought can be found in various spiritual movements and philosophies, a testament to its enduring appeal and the timeless quest for deeper understanding.

In exploring the world of Gnosticism, we are invited to question, to seek, and to wonder. It serves as a reminder that the journey of faith is as much inward as it is outward, and that in the depths of mystery, there often lies profound truth.

The Apocryphal Texts: An Overview

The term "apocryphal" often evokes a sense of mystery, of hidden or forbidden texts that lie just outside the boundaries of accepted canon. Derived from the Greek word "apokryphos," meaning "hidden" or "obscure," the Apocryphal texts are a collection of ancient writings that, for various reasons, did not find their way into the canonical Bible, the collection of books recognized by mainstream Christian denominations as divinely inspired.

But what exactly are these texts? The Apocryphal writings encompass a wide range of genres, from gospels and epistles to histories and prophecies. They were written over several centuries, spanning from the last few centuries BCE to the early centuries CE. Some of these texts, like the Book of Tobit or the Wisdom of Sirach, are deeply spiritual and offer moral guidance. Others, like the Gospel of Mary or the Acts of Peter, provide alternative perspectives on familiar biblical figures and events.

The reasons for the exclusion of these texts from the canonical Bible are multifaceted. One primary reason is the issue of authenticity. The early Church fathers, in their efforts to consolidate Christian doctrine and practice, sought writings that they believed had apostolic origins or were closely linked to the apostles. Many of the Apocryphal texts, despite their spiritual insights, could not be traced back to the apostolic era or were believed to have been written under pseudonyms.

Another significant factor was theological consistency. The early Christian Church, while diverse in many of its beliefs and practices, was also engaged in defining orthodoxy – the set of beliefs deemed correct – and distinguishing it from heresy. Some Apocryphal writings contained ideas or narratives that were at odds with the emerging orthodox Christian doctrine. For instance, certain texts might have Gnostic leanings or present views on Christ's nature that diverged from the developing consensus.

Furthermore, the process of canonization – the official recognition of texts as divinely inspired – was influenced by the practical needs of the early Christian communities.

Texts that were widely read in liturgical settings, that resonated with the faithful, and that were useful for catechesis, or religious instruction, had a better chance of being canonized.

It's essential to understand that the exclusion of these texts from the canon does not necessarily diminish their spiritual or historical value. Many of the Apocryphal writings provide invaluable insights into the diverse beliefs, practices, and struggles of early Christian communities. They reflect the richness of the Christian tradition and the myriad ways in which the message of Christ was understood and interpreted.

In today's context, as scholars and spiritual seekers alike delve into the Apocryphal texts, they often find a treasure trove of wisdom, alternative narratives, and theological reflections. These texts invite us to broaden our understanding of early Christianity and to appreciate the depth and diversity of the Christian heritage.

Judas Iscariot: The Biblical Account

Judas Iscariot stands as one of the most enigmatic and controversial figures in the New Testament. His name, forever linked with betrayal, has become synonymous with treachery in the annals of history. Yet, to truly understand Judas, one must delve into the biblical narratives, examining his portrayal in the New Testament and the complex web of motivations and interpretations surrounding his fateful act.

Judas in the New Testament

In the New Testament, Judas is introduced as one of the twelve disciples chosen by Jesus to accompany him in his ministry. While the Gospels of Matthew, Mark, Luke, and John each provide their own account of Judas's actions and fate, certain commonalities emerge. He is consistently identified as the one who would betray Jesus, setting into motion the events leading to the crucifixion.

Yet, beyond this act of betrayal, the Gospels offer glimpses into Judas's character and his relationship with Jesus. In John's Gospel, Judas is depicted as the keeper of the money bag for the disciples, and on one occasion, he criticizes Mary of Bethany for anointing Jesus with expensive perfume, suggesting the money could have been better spent on the poor. John, however, adds a critical note, suggesting Judas's concern was not for the poor but because he used to steal from the common fund.

The Betrayal of Jesus: Motivations and Interpretations
The act of betraying Jesus to the religious authorities is the defining moment in Judas's narrative. The Gospels provide varying details about this event. In Matthew, Judas agrees to betray Jesus for thirty pieces of silver, the price of a slave. In Luke and John, there are hints of satanic influence, with references to Satan entering Judas.

The motivations behind Judas's betrayal have been a subject of speculation and debate for centuries. Was it greed that drove him, as suggested by the thirty pieces of silver?

Or was it disillusionment, perhaps stemming from a belief that Jesus would not fulfill the messianic expectations of liberating Israel from Roman rule? Some theologians have even posited that Judas's actions were a misguided attempt to force Jesus's hand, to push him into manifesting his divine power and establishing his kingdom on earth.

The aftermath of the betrayal is equally shrouded in mystery and tragedy. Overwhelmed by guilt, Matthew's Gospel recounts that Judas tried to return the blood money and, when rebuffed, threw it into the temple before going out to hang himself. This act of despair contrasts sharply with Peter's denial of Jesus, another form of betrayal, yet one followed by repentance and forgiveness.

The figure of Judas Iscariot challenges us to grapple with complex questions of free will, destiny, and redemption. While his betrayal set the stage for the crucifixion and the subsequent resurrection, it also serves as a poignant reminder of the human capacity for choice, with all its inherent frailties and consequences. Through the ages, theologians, artists, and writers have sought to understand and interpret Judas's actions, finding in his story a reflection of the broader human experience, with its interplay of light and shadow, loyalty, and betrayal.

The Gospel of Judas: A Detailed Analysis

The Gospel of Judas, a text that lay hidden for centuries, offers a radically different perspective on familiar biblical events and characters. Unlike the canonical Gospels of the New Testament, which cast Judas Iscariot in the role of the betrayer, this Gospel presents him in a more favorable light, revealing a deeper, more intimate relationship with Jesus and challenging traditional Christian narratives.

The Narrative and Teachings of the Gospel

The Gospel of Judas is not a linear narrative like some of the canonical Gospels. Instead, it is a series of dialogues between Jesus and Judas, interspersed with visions and teachings that delve into Gnostic cosmology and theology.

Central to the Gospel is the Gnostic belief in a supreme, unknowable God and the existence of a divine realm populated by spiritual beings called "aeons." The material world, in Gnostic thought, is the creation of a lesser deity, the demiurge, and is inherently flawed. Humanity's spiritual essence, a divine spark, is trapped in this material realm, and salvation lies in awakening to this inner divinity and transcending the physical world.

Jesus, in the Gospel of Judas, is portrayed as a teacher of secret wisdom, imparting knowledge that is not shared with the other disciples. He speaks of the nature of the divine realm, the origins of the universe, and the destiny of souls. The Gospel emphasizes the idea that only a select few are capable of understanding these mysteries, and Judas is chosen for this revelation.

The Portrayal of Judas and His Relationship with Jesus

The relationship between Jesus and Judas is central to the Gospel. Far from the traitor of Christian tradition, Judas here is depicted as Jesus's confidant, chosen to receive teachings not shared with the other disciples. Jesus sees in Judas the potential to understand the deeper mysteries of existence, and their dialogues reflect a mutual respect and intimacy.

In one particularly poignant passage, Jesus tells Judas, "You will exceed all of them. For you will sacrifice the man that clothes me." This cryptic statement alludes to the idea that Judas's act of betrayal will lead to Jesus's crucifixion and, consequently, the shedding of his physical form, allowing his spiritual essence to return to the divine realm.

However, this privileged position also isolates Judas. He is set apart from the other disciples, bearing the weight of knowledge that they cannot comprehend. The Gospel hints at the inner turmoil and conflict Judas experiences, torn between his loyalty to Jesus and the profound implications of the role he is destined to play.

The Gospel of Judas challenges readers to reconsider long-held beliefs and assumptions. By presenting Judas not as a villain but as a key player in a cosmic revelation, it invites reflection on themes of destiny, free will, and the nature of salvation. It is a testament to the rich tapestry of early Christian thought and the diverse ways in which the story of Jesus and his disciples was understood and interpreted.

Contrasting Judas: Canonical Gospels vs. The Gospel of Judas

The figure of Judas Iscariot, as presented in the canonical Gospels and the Gospel of Judas, offers a fascinating study in contrast. These differing portrayals not only shed light on the diverse interpretations of early Christian communities but also raise profound theological questions about the nature of betrayal, divine purpose, and the complexities of human agency.

How the Portrayal of Judas Differs

In the canonical Gospels of Matthew, Mark, Luke, and John, Judas is primarily known for his act of betrayal. He is the disciple who, for thirty pieces of silver, hands Jesus over to the religious authorities, setting into motion the events that lead to the crucifixion. While the specifics vary slightly across the Gospels—such as his motivations or the manner of his death—the overarching narrative paints Judas as the quintessential traitor. His name becomes synonymous with betrayal, and his legacy is one of infamy.

The Gospel of Judas, on the other hand, offers a radical departure from this narrative. Instead of the betrayer, Judas emerges as a chosen confidant, privy to teachings and mysteries that Jesus does not share with the other disciples. Their dialogues reveal a deeper, more nuanced relationship, with Jesus recognizing in Judas the capacity to understand the spiritual truths he imparts. The act of betrayal, rather than a manifestation of greed or treachery, is framed as a necessary step in the larger cosmic event that is happening, facilitating Jesus's return to the divine realm.

Theological Implications of These Differences

The contrasting portrayals of Judas have profound theological implications that challenge and expand traditional Christian understandings:

Nature of Betrayal: In the canonical Gospels, Judas's betrayal is a moral failing, a deliberate choice to turn against Jesus. In the Gospel of Judas, this act takes on a more complex dimension. If Judas's actions are part of a divine plan, can they truly be considered a betrayal? This raises questions about the nature of free will, destiny, and the parameters of moral agency.

Concept of Salvation: The Gospel of Judas, with its Gnostic leanings, presents salvation as an awakening to inner divinity and a transcendence of the material world. This stands in contrast to the canonical view of salvation through faith in Jesus's sacrifice and resurrection. The role Judas plays in these differing narratives of salvation underscores the diverse theological interpretations of early Christian communities.

Re-evaluation of Judas: If Judas is not the villain but a pivotal player in a divine plan, it necessitates a re-evaluation of his character and legacy. It challenges the binary of good and evil, inviting a more compassionate and nuanced understanding of human actions and motivations.

Authority and Canon: The very existence of the Gospel of Judas and its contrasting narrative raises questions about the formation of the Christian canon. Who decides which texts are "authentic" or "heretical"? How do power dynamics, theological debates, and historical contexts influence these decisions?

In conclusion, the contrasting portrayals of Judas Iscariot in the canonical Gospels and the Gospel of Judas offer more than just differing narratives. They open a window into the rich and diverse world of early Christian thought, prompting reflection on foundational theological concepts and the ever-evolving nature of religious understanding.

The Cosmic Drama: Gnostic Creation Myths

Gnosticism, with its intricate cosmologies and profound spiritual insights, presents a view of the universe that is both captivating and challenging. At the heart of Gnostic thought lies a series of creation myths that diverge significantly from the more familiar Judeo-Christian narratives. These myths, rich in symbolism and allegory, paint a picture of a universe born out of divine emanations, cosmic disruptions, and the interplay between light and darkness.

The Gnostic View of Creation and the Material World

In Gnostic cosmology, the universe's origin is rooted in a realm that is beyond comprehension, often referred to as the Pleroma or "fullness." This is the domain of the supreme, unknowable God, an entity that transcends all concepts and definitions. From this divine source emanate a series of spiritual beings or "aeons," each representing facets of the divine essence. These aeons exist in harmonious pairs, or "syzygies," and their interactions give rise to further spiritual realities. However, this harmony is disrupted when one of the aeons, often named Sophia (meaning "wisdom"), attempts to know or comprehend the unknowable God. This act of overreaching results in a rupture, leading to the creation of a flawed, lower realm. Sophia's misguided desire produces an imperfect entity, separate from the divine fullness of the Pleroma.

This lower realm, the material world, is seen by the Gnostics as a place of entrapment and ignorance.

The divine spark, a remnant of the Pleroma, is imprisoned within human beings, ensnared by the physical body and the illusory nature of the material universe. Salvation, in Gnostic thought, involves awakening to this inner divinity and seeking a return to the Pleroma, transcending the confines of the material world.

The Role of the Demiurge
Central to the Gnostic creation myth is the figure of the demiurge, a powerful being responsible for crafting the material world. Born from the disruptions in the Pleroma and often identified as the offspring of Sophia, the demiurge is ignorant of the higher divine realm from which he originates. Believing himself to be the sole deity, he crafts the material universe in imitation of the Pleroma, albeit in a flawed and imperfect manner.

The demiurge, in many Gnostic texts, is associated with the God of the Old Testament. He is depicted as a jealous and vengeful deity, demanding worship, and obedience from humanity. Under his dominion are a host of lesser entities, often referred to as "archons," who assist in governing the material realm and keeping humanity in a state of ignorance and subservience.

The portrayal of the demiurge challenges traditional Judeo-Christian understandings of God. Instead of a benevolent creator, the demiurge is an imposter, a being who, in his ignorance, keeps humanity bound to the material world and away from their true spiritual nature.

In conclusion, the Gnostic creation myths offer a complex and nuanced view of the universe's origins and the nature of divinity. They speak of a cosmic drama, where divine aspirations and disruptions give rise to a multi-layered reality. Through these myths, Gnosticism invites individuals to embark on a spiritual journey, to seek knowledge, and to transcend the illusory barriers of the material world, ultimately returning to the divine source from which all things emanate.

The Role of Sacrifice in Gnostic Thought

Sacrifice, as a concept and practice, has been central to many religious traditions, including Christianity. However, Gnostic thought, with its distinctive cosmology and theology, offers a unique perspective on the role and meaning of sacrifice, particularly in relation to the crucifixion of Jesus. This perspective not only critiques mainstream Christian beliefs but also provides an alternative understanding of Jesus' sacrifice, especially as presented in texts like the Gospel of Judas.

The Critique of Mainstream Christian Beliefs

In mainstream Christian doctrine, the crucifixion of Jesus is seen as a redemptive act. Jesus, as the Son of God, sacrifices himself for the sins of humanity, offering salvation to all who believe in him. This act of self-sacrifice is central to Christian soteriology and is commemorated in rituals like the Eucharist.

Gnostic thought, however, often critiques this interpretation. From a Gnostic perspective, the material world, including its rituals and institutions, is inherently flawed and distant from the true divine realm. Consequently, traditional understandings of sacrifice, which emphasize the physical act of Jesus' crucifixion, are seen as missing the deeper, spiritual significance of the event. For the Gnostics, salvation doesn't come from a physical act but from gnosis – the profound, transformative knowledge of one's divine nature and the cosmos's true structure.

The True Meaning of Jesus' Sacrifice According to the Gospel of Judas

The Gospel of Judas, one of the most intriguing Gnostic texts, offers a radical reinterpretation of Jesus' sacrifice. In this text, Jesus' death is not a redemptive act to atone for humanity's sins. Instead, it is a necessary step in a cosmic drama, facilitating his release from the material body and his return to the divine realm.

Judas, rather than being the villainous betrayer, plays a crucial role in this process. He is chosen by Jesus to assist in this liberation. The act of "betrayal" is, in fact, an act of obedience to Jesus' will, a necessary step to free the divine spirit from the confines of the material world.

In the Gospel of Judas, Jesus often speaks critically of the other disciples' lack of understanding and their adherence to ritualistic practices, which he deems as misguided. The true sacrifice is not the shedding of physical blood but the shedding of ignorance, the transcendence of the material realm, and the realization of one's true, divine nature.

In this context, Jesus' sacrifice becomes a symbol of the Gnostic believer's journey. Just as Jesus transcends the material world, so too must the believer seek to rise above the physical realm's illusions, seeking the true knowledge that leads to spiritual liberation.

In conclusion, the role of sacrifice in Gnostic thought challenges traditional Christian interpretations, offering a more inward, mystical understanding of Jesus' crucifixion. It speaks to a spiritual journey of awakening, where the true sacrifice lies in letting go of material attachments and embracing one's divine essence.

The Secret Knowledge: Gnostic Teachings and Rituals

Gnosticism, with its emphasis on esoteric knowledge and spiritual enlightenment, stands as a testament to the diverse tapestry of early Christian thought. Central to Gnostic belief is the concept of "gnosis", this secret knowledge, often revealed through teachings and rituals, provides a pathway to divine understanding and spiritual ascension.

The Mysteries Revealed to Judas

In the Gospel of Judas, Judas Iscariot is presented as a chosen confidant, privy to teachings that Jesus does not share with the other disciples. These teachings delve into the mysteries of the cosmos, the nature of the divine, and the path to spiritual liberation.

Jesus speaks to Judas of the divine realm, the Pleroma, where a supreme, unknowable God resides. He reveals the existence of various aeons, spiritual entities that emanate from this divine source. The Gospel delves into the complexities of Gnostic cosmology, detailing the creation of the material world, the role of the demiurge, and the inherent flaws of the physical realm.

Furthermore, Jesus imparts to Judas the knowledge of humanity's true nature. Beneath the physical exterior lies a divine spark, a fragment of the Pleroma trapped in the material world. The journey of the Gnostic believer is to recognize this inner divinity, to awaken to the truth of their spiritual essence, and to seek a return to the divine realm.

Gnostic Rituals and Their Significance

While the Gospel of Judas emphasizes teachings and revelations, Gnostic practice also encompassed a range of rituals that aimed to facilitate spiritual awakening and transformation. These rituals, often shrouded in secrecy, were integral to the Gnostic path to salvation.

Baptism: Much like in mainstream Christianity, baptism held significance in Gnostic practice. However, Gnostic baptism was not just a rite of initiation but a purification ritual. It symbolized the cleansing of the soul from the material world's impurities and the awakening of the inner divine spark.

Eucharist: The Gnostic Eucharist differed from the traditional Christian sacrament. While it involved the consumption of bread and wine, it was seen as a symbolic act of internalizing divine knowledge and mysteries, rather than commemorating Jesus' sacrifice.

Bridal Chamber: One of the more esoteric Gnostic rituals, the Bridal Chamber, symbolized the union of the soul with the divine. It represented the merging of the individual's spiritual essence with the greater cosmic reality, a profound mystical experience that marked a significant step in the believer's spiritual journey.

Prayers and Invocations: Gnostic rituals often included prayers, hymns, and invocations, calling upon various aeons and spiritual entities. These were not just acts of devotion but tools to attune the believer's consciousness to higher spiritual realities.

In conclusion, the secret knowledge of Gnostic teachings and rituals offers a window into a spiritual tradition that sought to transcend the material world's limitations and attain a profound union with the divine. Through teachings, as revealed to figures like Judas, and through sacred rituals, Gnosticism charted a path of inner transformation, leading the believer from ignorance to enlightenment, from darkness to light.

The Controversy: Early Church Reactions to Gnostic Texts

The emergence of Gnostic texts and beliefs in the early Christian era sparked significant controversy and debate within the burgeoning Christian community. As the Church sought to define its doctrines and solidify its identity, Gnostic teachings, with their alternative interpretations of Christian narratives and their emphasis on esoteric knowledge, posed a challenge to the developing orthodoxy. The reactions of the early Church to Gnosticism, marked by critiques from Church Fathers and efforts to suppress Gnostic beliefs, highlight the tensions and struggles of this formative period in Christian history.

The Church Fathers and Their Critiques

The Church Fathers, influential theologians, and leaders of the early Christian Church played a pivotal role in shaping Christian doctrine and practice. In their writings, many of these figures directly addressed and critiqued Gnostic beliefs:

Irenaeus of Lyons: One of the most vocal critics of Gnosticism, wrote a text named "Against Heresies," a comprehensive work that sought to refute Gnostic teachings. He argued that Gnostic beliefs deviated from the apostolic tradition and emphasized the importance of the Church's authority in preserving true Christian teachings.

Tertullian: As a prolific writer, Tertullian criticized Gnostic reliance on secret teachings and mysteries. He championed the idea of "rule of faith," a set of core Christian beliefs that stood in contrast to the shifting and diverse doctrines of Gnosticism.

Hippolytus of Rome: In his work "Refutation of All Heresies," Hippolytus detailed various Gnostic beliefs and practices, presenting them as deviations from true Christian faith. He particularly critiqued the Gnostic view of creation and the demiurge.

Clement of Alexandria: While he acknowledged the value of spiritual knowledge, he believed that true gnosis was in line with the Church's teachings and was accessible to all believers, not just a select few. These critiques often centered on a few key issues: the authenticity and authority of Gnostic texts versus the canonical scriptures, the nature of God and creation as presented in Gnostic cosmology, and the role of Jesus and the meaning of his teachings.

The Suppression of Gnostic Beliefs
As the early Church worked to consolidate its power and define its doctrines, there was a concerted effort to suppress beliefs and practices deemed heretical, including Gnosticism, such as:
Canon Formation: The process of determining which texts were considered divinely inspired and authoritative led to the exclusion of many Gnostic writings from the New Testament canon.

Councils and Creeds: Church councils, such as the Council of Nicaea, sought to establish orthodox Christian beliefs and practices. These councils often explicitly rejected Gnostic interpretations.

Persecution: Gnostic groups and individuals faced persecution, with their texts often confiscated and destroyed.

This suppression was not just theological but also political, as the Church sought to maintain its authority and cohesion.

Monasticism: The rise of Christian monasticism, with its emphasis on asceticism and communal living, also countered Gnostic individualism and the pursuit of secret knowledge.

In conclusion, the early Church's reactions to Gnostic texts and beliefs reflect the broader struggles of a religious community seeking to define itself in a diverse and often contentious spiritual landscape. The critiques of the Church Fathers and the efforts to suppress Gnostic beliefs underscore the challenges posed by Gnosticism and the Church's determination to establish a unified and orthodox Christian identity.

The Rediscovery: The Modern Discovery of the Gospel of Judas

For centuries, the Gospel of Judas remained a shadowy presence in Christian history, known primarily through the critiques of early Church Fathers. However, the modern era brought with it a groundbreaking discovery that would shed new light on this enigmatic text, offering scholars and theologians a chance to engage directly with its content. The rediscovery of the Gospel of Judas, with its tale of manuscript discovery and the subsequent challenges of translation and interpretation, adds a fascinating chapter to the annals of biblical archaeology and scholarship.

The Story of the Manuscript's Discovery

The modern journey of the Gospel of Judas began in the 1970s in the desert near El Minya, Egypt. Here, local farmers stumbled upon a bound codex containing several ancient texts. Unaware of its significance, the manuscript changed hands multiple times, often in shadowy circumstances involving antiquities dealers and black-market traders. The codex faced potential damage due to mishandling, environmental conditions, and even attempts to increase its market value by dividing pages.

It wasn't until the early 2000s that the manuscript, now recognized as a significant Gnostic text, came to the attention of scholars and institutions dedicated to preserving and studying ancient writings. With the involvement of the Maecenas Foundation for Ancient Art and the National Geographic Society, scholars began to conserve, study, and ultimately share the Gospel of Judas with the world.

The Challenges of Translation and Interpretation

Given the age of the manuscript and the conditions it had endured, translating, and interpreting the Gospel of Judas presented a formidable challenge:

In fact, the codex, having suffered from both time and mishandling, was fragmented in many places. This meant that scholars had to painstakingly piece together sections, often working with tiny fragments, to reconstruct the text.

The manuscript was also written in Coptic, an ancient Egyptian language. While there are experts in Coptic, the nuances of the language, especially in religious texts, required careful and collaborative translation efforts.

To accurately interpret the Gospel of Judas, scholars needed a deep understanding of Gnostic beliefs, cosmology, and terminology. The text is replete with references to Gnostic concepts, and understanding these was crucial to capturing its essence.

The Gospel of Judas was compared with other Gnostic texts and early Christian writings to ensure accurate translation and to place it in its historical and theological context.

As with any significant religious discovery, the Gospel of Judas sparked debates among scholars, theologians, and the broader public. Questions about its authenticity, its implications for Christian theology, and its portrayal of Judas led to vibrant discussions in academic and religious circles.

In conclusion, the modern rediscovery of the Gospel of Judas is a testament to the enduring quest for knowledge and understanding of humanity's spiritual heritage.

The journey of the manuscript, from its ancient origins to its modern unveiling, underscores the complexities and challenges of engaging with the past, even as it offers new insights into age-old questions of faith, betrayal, and redemption.

The Gospel's Authenticity: Scholarly Debates

The discovery of the Gospel of Judas ignited a firestorm of interest, not just among theologians and historians, but also in the broader public. Central to the discussions surrounding this text was the question of its authenticity. Was this truly an ancient Christian or Gnostic text that offered a different perspective on Judas Iscariot, or was it a more recent fabrication or forgery? The debates around this question have profound implications for our understanding of early Christian history and the diverse beliefs that flourished during its formative years.

Arguments for the Gospel's Authenticity

They used physical analysis to prove its authenticity. Scientific tests, including radiocarbon dating of the papyrus and ink analysis, indicated that the Gospel of Judas likely dates back to the 3rd or 4th century AD. This places the physical manuscript within the timeframe of other known Gnostic texts.

In addition, the language and style of the Gospel of Judas, written in Coptic, are consistent with other texts from the same period. The use of certain phrases, terms, and linguistic structures aligns with what scholars would expect from an ancient Gnostic text.

Another proof of its authenticity can be found in ancient texts. Early Christian writers, such as Irenaeus of Lyons in the 2nd century AD, made reference to a "Gospel of Judas." While it's not definitive proof, it suggests that a text by this name, which portrayed Judas in a positive light, was known in early Christian circles.

Arguments Against the Gospel's Authenticity
There are also some arguments against the Gospel's authenticity. While the physical manuscript might date back to the 3rd or 4th century, it could be a copy of an earlier text, or a later fabrication based on older traditions. Without additional copies or references, it's challenging to pinpoint its origins definitively.

Also, some scholars argue that the Gospel of Judas contains theological ideas or interpretations that don't align neatly with what is known about Gnostic beliefs or early Christian thought. Given the potential value and significance of such a text, questions arose about the possibility of forgery, especially in the lucrative market for biblical antiquities. Some skeptics wondered if the Gospel was created or altered to fit a particular narrative or agenda.

The Implications for Christian History
The authenticity debate surrounding the Gospel of Judas has broader implications for our understanding of Christian history:
If authentic, the Gospel of Judas underscores the rich diversity of beliefs and interpretations in early Christianity. It challenges the monolithic view of early Christian thought and highlights the debates and tensions within the early Church. Also, an authentic Gospel of Judas would necessitate a re-examination of Judas Iscariot's role in the Christian narrative. It would offer a counter-narrative to the traditional portrayal of Judas as a betrayer, prompting discussions on themes of destiny, free will, and divine purpose.
The Gospel's discovery would also shed light on the process of canon formation in early Christianity. It would raise questions about which texts were included in the New Testament, which were excluded, and why.
In conclusion, the debates surrounding the authenticity of the Gospel of Judas are not just academic exercises. They touch on fundamental questions about the nature of faith, the complexities of history, and the ever-evolving understanding of religious truths. Whether viewed as an authentic ancient text or a subject of skepticism, the Gospel of Judas undeniably adds a rich layer to the tapestry of Christian history and thought.

The Role of Women in Gnostic Texts

Gnosticism, with its diverse range of texts and teachings, offers a unique lens through which to explore the role and portrayal of women in early Christian thought. Unlike many mainstream Christian texts of the time, which often reflected the patriarchal structures of the surrounding society, Gnostic writings frequently presented women in more prominent and nuanced roles. This emphasis on female figures, particularly figures like Mary Magdalene, not only highlights the distinctiveness of Gnostic beliefs but also suggests a potential challenge to the prevailing gender norms of the era.

The Portrayal of Mary Magdalene and Other Female Figures

In Gnostic texts, Mary Magdalene is often depicted as one of Jesus' closest disciples, privy to teachings and insights not shared with others. The Gospel of Mary, a Gnostic text attributed to Mary Magdalene, presents her as a spiritual leader, sharing revelations she received from Jesus with the other disciples. This portrayal stands in stark contrast to the more limited role she occupies in the canonical Gospels, where she is primarily known as a repentant sinner and witness to the resurrection.

A central figure in many Gnostic cosmologies, Sophia, whose name means "wisdom" in Greek, is often described as a divine emanation or aeon. Her story, which involves a fall from the divine realm and a subsequent redemption, is symbolic of the human soul's journey in Gnostic thought. As a female representation of divine wisdom, Sophia's narrative underscores the importance of feminine aspects in the Gnostic understanding of the divine.

Gnostic texts also mention other female figures, such as Salome and Martha, giving them roles and significance that go beyond their portrayals in canonical scriptures. These women are often depicted as seekers of knowledge, challenging traditional norms, and engaging in theological discussions.

Gnosticism's Potential Challenge to Patriarchal Structures

Gnostic beliefs emphasize the divine spark within every individual, regardless of gender. This inherent spiritual potential challenges the gender hierarchies prevalent in many religious and societal structures of the time. In Gnostic communities, women could potentially serve as spiritual leaders, teachers, and prophets.

Some Gnostic texts also offer alternative interpretations of the Genesis creation narrative. Instead of viewing Eve's actions in the Garden of Eden as the cause of humanity's downfall, these interpretations celebrate her pursuit of knowledge and see her as a precursor to the Gnostic seeker.

The Gnostic emphasis on personal revelation and inner knowledge often stood in opposition to the hierarchical structures of the early Church. By valuing the insights and experiences of women, Gnosticism implicitly challenged the male-dominated leadership of the Church.

In conclusion, the role of women in Gnostic texts provides a window into the broader theological and social debates of the early Christian era. The prominence of figures like Mary Magdalene and Sophia, coupled with the Gnostic emphasis on inner knowledge and spiritual equality, suggests a tradition that, in many ways, stood in contrast to the patriarchal norms of its time. Whether seen as a direct challenge or a parallel perspective, the portrayal of women in Gnostic writings adds depth and complexity to our understanding of early Christian thought and the place of women within it.

The Gospel of Judas in Popular Culture

The discovery and subsequent publication of the Gospel of Judas captured the imagination of the public, scholars, and artists alike. This alternative narrative, which portrayed one of Christianity's most vilified figures in a new light, resonated deeply in a culture fascinated by hidden truths, reinterpretations, and the blending of historical fact with creative fiction. As a result, the Gospel of Judas has left a significant imprint on various facets of popular culture, from literature and art to film and beyond.

Modern Interpretations and Adaptations

The Gospel of Judas has inspired numerous authors to explore the character of Judas Iscariot in greater depth. Novels, short stories, and poems have delved into the psyche of Judas, often drawing from the Gnostic portrayal to craft a more nuanced and sympathetic character. These literary explorations often grapple with themes of betrayal, redemption, and the nature of good and evil.

The stage has also seen adaptations that bring the Gospel of Judas to life, often juxtaposing the Gnostic narrative with the canonical Gospel accounts. These performances challenge audiences to reconsider their perceptions of Judas and question the nature of historical truth and religious dogma.

Composers and songwriters, intrigued by the Gospel's themes, have incorporated its narratives and motifs into their works. From classical compositions to modern rock ballads, the story of Judas, as presented in the Gnostic text, has found its way into musical interpretations that resonate with contemporary audiences.

The Gospel's Influence on Art, Literature, and Film

Even painters and sculptors have been drawn to the Gospel of Judas, using its narrative to craft artworks that challenge traditional Christian iconography. These pieces often depict Judas in a more contemplative or even saintly light, contrasting starkly with the treacherous figure of mainstream Christian art.

Beyond direct adaptations, the Gospel of Judas has influenced broader literary themes. The idea of hidden gospels, suppressed truths, and religious conspiracies has become a popular trope in mystery and thriller genres, with the Gospel of Judas serving as a touchstone for these narratives.

The world of cinema has not remained untouched by the Gospel's allure. Documentaries have explored its discovery, significance, and impact, while fictional films have woven its narrative into plots that span historical drama, religious intrigue, and even supernatural thriller genres. Television series, especially those delving into religious mysteries or alternative histories, have also referenced or incorporated elements from the Gospel of Judas.

In conclusion, the Gospel of Judas, with its alternative portrayal of one of history's most enigmatic figures, has permeated popular culture in diverse and profound ways. Its influence is a testament to the enduring fascination with hidden truths and the power of narrative to challenge, inspire, and transform. Whether embraced as a genuine religious text or as a compelling piece of historical fiction, the Gospel of Judas continues to inspire artists, writers, and creators, leaving an indelible mark on the cultural landscape.

Comparing Other Gnostic Texts: The Gospel of Thomas, Mary, and Philip

The Gnostic texts, discovered in various locations and at different times, offer a rich tapestry of alternative Christian thought. While the Gospel of Judas has garnered significant attention due to its unique portrayal of Judas Iscariot, other Gnostic gospels, such as those of Thomas, Mary, and Philip, are equally intriguing and provide valuable insights into early Christian heterodoxy. By comparing these texts, we can discern common themes that characterize Gnostic beliefs, as well as the distinct nuances that each gospel brings to the fore.

The Gospel of Thomas

The Gospel of Thomas is a collection of sayings attributed to Jesus. Unlike the canonical gospels, it lacks a narrative structure and focuses solely on the teachings, many of which are esoteric in nature.

Like other Gnostic texts, the Gospel of Thomas emphasizes personal insight and the quest for spiritual knowledge. Several sayings suggest that the kingdom of God is within the individual and that understanding Jesus' words leads to eternal life.

In particular, the Gospel of Thomas stands out for its lack of narrative. It doesn't delve into the events of Jesus' life, his crucifixion, or resurrection. Instead, it presents a more mystical approach to his teachings.

The Gospel of Mary

This gospel offers insights into the teachings of Jesus as relayed by Mary Magdalene. It delves into post-resurrection dialogues between Mary and the other disciples and emphasizes her role as a prominent disciple.

The Gospel of Mary, like other Gnostic texts, underscores the concept of salvation through knowledge. It also touches upon the ascent of the soul, overcoming various challenges to reach higher spiritual realms.

In particular, the gospel elevates Mary Magdalene's status, presenting her as a source of wisdom and even causing tension with other disciples, notably Peter, due to her profound insights. This portrayal challenges traditional Christian narratives that often sideline her role.

The Gospel of Philip

The Gospel of Philip is a compilation of meditations and reflections on Christian rites, such as baptism and the Eucharist, as well as on the nature of the divine and the relationship between Jesus and his followers.

The text delves into the symbolic meanings behind Christian rituals, aligning with Gnostic thought that emphasizes the inner, mystical experience over the outer, ritualistic one. It also touches upon the concept of Jesus as the "bridal chamber," symbolizing the union of the soul with the divine.

The Gospel of Philip is notable for its exploration of sacraments and its allegorical interpretations. It also contains references to Mary Magdalene's close relationship with Jesus, suggesting a deeper spiritual intimacy.

Common Themes and Differences Across the Gospels

There are a lot of common themes among all these gospels, such as.

Inner Revelation: All these gospels emphasize personal spiritual insight over traditional religious dogma.

Elevation of Marginalized Figures: Figures like Mary Magdalene are given more prominent roles, challenging mainstream Christian narratives.

Mystical Union: The texts frequently allude to the idea of becoming one with the divine, transcending the physical realm.

There are also some differences, like the ones listed below.

Narrative Structure: While the Gospel of Thomas is a collection of sayings, the Gospels of Mary and Philip offer more narrative elements and dialogues.

Focus on Rituals: The Gospel of Philip stands out for its detailed exploration of Christian sacraments from a Gnostic perspective.

In conclusion, while the Gnostic gospels share overarching themes that reflect their distinct spiritual perspective, each text offers unique insights and emphases, enriching our understanding of early Christian diversity and thought.

The Legacy of the Gospel of Judas

The Gospel of Judas, with its alternative portrayal of one of Christianity's most infamous figures, has left an indelible mark on the landscape of religious scholarship and spiritual exploration. Its rediscovery and subsequent analysis have not only ignited debates among theologians and historians but have also resonated with modern spiritual seekers, particularly those aligned with Gnostic movements. The legacy of this gospel is multifaceted, challenging long-held beliefs and inspiring a reevaluation of early Christian diversity.

How the Gospel Challenges Traditional Christian Beliefs

At the heart of the Gospel of Judas is a radical reinterpretation of Judas Iscariot. Far from the traitor vilified in the canonical gospels, Judas emerges as a chosen disciple, entrusted with a special mission by Jesus. This portrayal challenges the traditional narrative of betrayal and suggests a more complex relationship between Jesus and Judas. The Gospel of Judas, in line with other Gnostic texts, emphasizes personal spiritual knowledge (gnosis) as the path to salvation. This stands in contrast to mainstream Christian doctrines that prioritize faith in Jesus' sacrificial death and resurrection.

The gospel contains implicit critiques of the apostles and, by extension, the early Church leadership. It suggests that they lacked a deeper understanding of Jesus' teachings, a claim that challenges the foundational authority of the Church.

Moreover, the Gospel of Judas presents a distinct cosmology, with references to multiple heavens and divine beings. This cosmological framework diverges from traditional Christian views of creation and the nature of the divine.

Its Impact on Modern Gnostic Movements

The discovery of the Gospel of Judas, along with other texts from the Nag Hammadi library, has provided modern Gnostic movements with tangible evidence of their historical roots. These texts validate certain Gnostic beliefs and practices, emphasizing the movement's early Christian origins.

The gospel's themes of inner revelation, spiritual ascent, and the quest for hidden knowledge resonate with many modern spiritual seekers. Its teachings inspire a personal, experiential approach to spirituality, encouraging individuals to seek their own truths.

In addition, the Gospel of Judas has facilitated conversations between mainstream Christian denominations and Gnostic movements. While differences remain, the text has opened avenues for dialogue and mutual exploration.

Beyond strictly religious circles, the Gospel of Judas has captured the imagination of the broader public. Its themes of betrayal, redemption, and hidden truths align with contemporary cultural narratives, making it a point of reference in discussions about religious history and spiritual exploration.

In conclusion, the legacy of the Gospel of Judas extends far beyond its pages. It challenges traditional Christian beliefs, prompting a reevaluation of long-held narratives and doctrines. Simultaneously, it invigorates modern Gnostic movements and spiritual seekers, serving as a testament to the rich tapestry of early Christian thought and its enduring impact on the spiritual landscape.

The Future of Gnostic Studies
The field of Gnostic studies, invigorated by the discovery of texts like the Gospel of Judas and the Nag Hammadi library, stands at an exciting juncture. As scholars delve deeper into these ancient writings, they uncover layers of meaning, historical context, and theological nuance. The future of Gnostic studies promises to be a dynamic blend of rigorous scholarship, interdisciplinary collaboration, and the tantalizing potential for new discoveries.

Current Research and Areas of Interest
With the availability of more Gnostic texts, scholars are engaged in detailed textual analysis, comparing different manuscripts, studying linguistic nuances, and exploring theological themes. This meticulous work sheds light on the evolution of Gnostic thought and its intersections with other early Christian movements.
Understanding the socio-political and cultural contexts in which Gnostic texts were written is crucial. Researchers are examining the historical circumstances that might have influenced Gnostic beliefs, from Roman persecution to interactions with other religious traditions.
Also, as seen in texts like the Gospel of Mary, Gnostic writings often offer a different perspective on the roles and statuses of women in early Christian communities. Scholars are keenly interested in exploring these portrayals and their implications for understanding gender dynamics in ancient religious settings.
Gnostic beliefs and texts don't exist in isolation. Researchers are increasingly interested in the interactions between Gnostic Christians, mainstream Christian groups, and other religious traditions of the time, such as Judaism and Greco-Roman religions.
The influence of ancient Gnostic beliefs on contemporary spiritual movements is a growing area of interest. Scholars are studying how modern groups interpret and adapt Gnostic teachings, and how these interpretations compare with historical understandings.

The Potential for New Discoveries

The discovery of the Nag Hammadi library and the Gospel of Judas came from archaeological digs. As excavations continue in regions historically significant for early Christianity, there's always the potential to unearth more manuscripts or artifacts that shed light on Gnostic beliefs.

Also, modern technology, from imaging techniques that can read faded manuscripts to digital platforms that facilitate global collaboration, is revolutionizing the field of Gnostic studies. These tools can uncover previously inaccessible information and foster collaborative research efforts.

As scholars approach known texts with fresh perspectives and methodologies, there's potential for new interpretations and insights. What was once considered a settled understanding can be reinvigorated with novel interpretations.

We can also take in account the increasing interest in Gnostic studies among the general public, fueled by media coverage and popular culture, may lead to crowd-sourced initiatives, amateur discoveries, and a democratization of research.

In conclusion, the future of Gnostic studies is bright, characterized by deepening scholarship, interdisciplinary collaboration, and the ever-present potential for groundbreaking discoveries. As researchers continue to explore the rich tapestry of Gnostic thought, they not only illuminate the past but also engage with contemporary questions about spirituality, identity, and the nature of belief.

Reflections: Personal Journeys with the Gospel of Judas

The Gospel of Judas, with its alternative narrative and profound theological implications, has not only been a subject of academic interest but has also deeply touched the lives of many who have encountered it. From scholars who have dedicated their careers to its study, to lay readers seeking spiritual insights, the text has inspired introspection, debate, and transformative experiences. Delving into these personal journeys offers a glimpse into the profound impact that ancient writings can have on contemporary lives.

Testimonies from Modern Readers and Scholars

For many scholars, the Gospel of Judas is more than just an ancient manuscript; it's a puzzle waiting to be deciphered. Dr. Elaine Pagels, a renowned scholar on Gnostic texts, speaks of the thrill of encountering such writings, which challenge and expand our understanding of early Christianity. For her and many others, the Gospel of Judas is a testament to the diversity of thought in the early Christian world, prompting a reevaluation of established narratives.

Lay readers, often on personal spiritual journeys, find in the Gospel of Judas a resonance with their own quests for deeper understanding. James, a reader from Canada, shares how the text's portrayal of Judas, not as a betrayer but as a confidant of Jesus, made him reconsider the nature of betrayal in his own life and the possibility of redemption.

Also, for practitioners of modern Gnostic movements, the Gospel of Judas is a validation of their beliefs. Sophia, a member of a Gnostic community in Australia, speaks of the profound connection she felt with the text, seeing in its teachings echoes of her own spiritual experiences and the emphasis on personal revelation.

Not all who are drawn to the Gospel of Judas come from a background of faith. Aaron, an agnostic from the UK, was intrigued by the historical and cultural significance of the text. Reading it, he found himself captivated by the philosophical questions it raised, prompting him to explore other religious writings and engage in discussions about the nature of faith and knowledge.

The Transformative Power of Gnostic Teachings

Central to Gnostic teachings is the idea of gnosis – knowledge that comes from within. For many, this emphasis on personal insight over external dogma is liberating, allowing for a more intimate and personal connection with the divine.

These texts tend to redefine the divine, in fact gnostic texts, including the Gospel of Judas, often present a more complex cosmology, with multiple divine beings and realms. This expanded view of the divine allows readers to explore different facets of spirituality and consider the nature of good and evil in more nuanced ways.

The Gnostic emphasis on seeking knowledge, even if it challenges established norms, resonates with many in our modern world, where questioning and critical thinking are valued. Engaging with Gnostic teachings empowers individuals to take charge of their spiritual journeys, seeking truths that resonate with their personal experiences. In conclusion, the Gospel of Judas, while ancient in origin, speaks to the timeless human quest for understanding, meaning, and connection. The reflections and journeys of those who engage with it underscore the enduring power of religious texts to inspire, challenge, and transform. Whether approached with scholarly rigor, spiritual fervor, or simple curiosity, the Gospel of Judas continues to touch lives, prompting introspection and discussions that bridge the past and the present.

Conclusion: Re-evaluating Judas and Early Christian History
The Gospel of Judas, with its profound reimagining of one of the most enigmatic figures in Christian lore, has catalyzed a broader reevaluation of early Christian history. Its revelations extend beyond the character of Judas Iscariot, prompting scholars, theologians, and spiritual seekers alike to delve deeper into the multifaceted tapestry of beliefs, narratives, and traditions that characterized the early Christian world. As we reflect on the lasting impact of this gospel and its place in the ongoing quest to understand early Christian beliefs, several key themes emerge.

The Lasting Impact of the Gospel of Judas
The Gospel of Judas turns the traditional story of Judas's betrayal on its head, presenting him not as a traitor but as a chosen disciple privy to esoteric teachings. This alternative portrayal invites readers to question long-held assumptions and consider the possibility of multiple, even conflicting, truths within early Christian traditions.
The Gospel of Judas underscores the rich diversity of thought and belief in the early Christian world. It serves as a reminder that what we now consider "orthodox" Christianity was once one of many competing interpretations, each vying for followers and legitimacy.

Also, the theological implications of the Gospel of Judas are profound. By emphasizing personal revelation and challenging traditional views of salvation, the gospel invites modern believers to engage in deeper theological reflections and discussions.

The Ongoing Quest for Understanding Early Christian Beliefs

The discovery of the Gospel of Judas has invigorated efforts to find other lost or suppressed Christian texts. Scholars and archaeologists continue to search for manuscripts that might offer further insights into the diverse beliefs of early Christian communities.

Understanding the Gospel of Judas and its context requires a melding of disciplines, from textual analysis and linguistics to history and archaeology. This interdisciplinary approach enriches our understanding and brings new perspectives to ancient texts.

The Gospel of Judas, while of historical significance, also resonates with many modern believers, especially those drawn to alternative spiritual paths or those questioning traditional religious narratives. Its teachings and themes continue to inspire discussions, debates, and spiritual explorations among contemporary audiences.

In wrapping up, the Gospel of Judas, far from being a mere historical curiosity, stands as a testament to the dynamic and diverse nature of early Christian thought. Its rediscovery and the subsequent debates it has sparked highlight the ever-evolving nature of religious belief and the human quest for spiritual understanding. As we continue to grapple with its teachings and implications, the Gospel of Judas serves as both a window into the past and a mirror reflecting our own spiritual journeys, challenges, and aspirations.

Gnostic and Apocryphal Gospel of Philip: A Deep Dive

The Significance of the Gospel of Philip in Gnostic Literature

Historical Context

The Gospel of Philip, like many Gnostic texts, emerged during a time of great theological diversity and debate within early Christianity. The 2nd and 3rd centuries CE saw a proliferation of Christian sects, each with its own interpretations of Jesus' teachings and the nature of salvation. The Gospel of Philip, with its unique blend of Christian doctrine and Gnostic cosmology, represents one of these alternative voices.

Unique Theological Insights

While many Gnostic texts focus on the cosmological narrative, detailing the creation of the world by a lesser god (the Demiurge) and the trapping of divine sparks in material bodies, the Gospel of Philip is more concerned with sacramental theology and spiritual transformation. It delves into the symbolic meanings of Christian rites like baptism and the Eucharist, offering a Gnostic interpretation that emphasizes personal gnosis (knowledge) and union with the divine.

Sacramental Theology

The Gospel of Philip provides a detailed exploration of the sacraments, especially the Bridal Chamber's rite. In orthodox Christianity, sacraments are outward signs of inward grace. In the Gospel of Philip, they become symbolic acts that facilitate the soul's return to the divine realm. The Bridal Chamber, in particular, symbolizes the soul's union with the divine, transcending the material world's limitations.

Mary Magdalene and the Divine Feminine

The Gospel of Philip is notable for its portrayal of Mary Magdalene as a close companion and confidante of Jesus. This portrayal challenges traditional Christian narratives that often marginalize or downplay her role. The text's emphasis on the divine feminine and spiritual union also sets it apart from other Gnostic writings, highlighting the importance of balance and unity in the spiritual journey.

Allegorical Interpretations

The Gospel of Philip is rich in allegory and symbolism. It often employs metaphorical language to convey deeper spiritual truths, urging readers to look beyond the literal and seek the hidden meanings. This allegorical approach is a hallmark of Gnostic literature, inviting readers to engage in a deeper, more personal exploration of the text.

Legacy and Influence

Despite not being included in the canonical New Testament, the Gospel of Philip has had a lasting impact on Christian mysticism and modern Gnostic movements. Its teachings on spiritual union, the divine feminine, and sacramental theology have resonated with many spiritual seekers, making it one of the most studied and revered Gnostic texts.

The Gospel of Philip holds a unique place in Gnostic literature. Its blend of Christian and Gnostic elements, its emphasis on sacramental theology, and its allegorical approach make it a rich and complex text that continues to inspire and challenge readers. Its significance lies not just in its historical context but in its timeless messages about the nature of the divine and the human soul's quest for spiritual enlightenment.

The Gospel of Philip: An Overview

Origins and Discovery

The Gospel of Philip is one of the texts discovered in 1945 near the town of Nag Hammadi in Upper Egypt. This collection, known as the Nag Hammadi library, comprises 13 codices containing over 50 texts, many of which are Gnostic in nature. The Gospel of Philip is written in Coptic, but it is believed to have been originally composed in Greek during the 2nd or 3rd century CE.

Structure and Content

Unlike the canonical gospels, which are primarily narrative, the Gospel of Philip is a collection of sayings, teachings, and reflections. It lacks a continuous narrative about Jesus' life, death, and resurrection. Instead, it offers a series of logia (sayings or teachings) and commentaries that delve into spiritual, theological, and sacramental topics.

Major Themes

Sacramental Theology: One of the most distinctive features of the Gospel of Philip is its focus on sacraments, particularly baptism, the Eucharist, and the Bridal Chamber. These rituals are seen not merely as symbolic acts but as transformative experiences that lead to spiritual enlightenment and union with the divine.

Spiritual Union and the Bridal Chamber: The concept of the Bridal Chamber is central to the Gospel of Philip. It symbolizes the spiritual union between the believer and the divine, transcending earthly marriages and pointing to a deeper, mystical union.

The Divine Feminine: The Gospel gives significant attention to female figures, most notably Mary Magdalene. It challenges traditional Christian views by presenting Mary as a close companion and spiritual confidante of Jesus.

Allegory and Symbolism: The text is rich in allegorical language, urging readers to seek deeper, hidden meanings behind the words. It emphasizes the importance of personal gnosis (knowledge) and spiritual insight over literal interpretations.

Creation and Redemption: Like other Gnostic texts, the Gospel of Philip presents a distinct view of creation, where the material world is seen as flawed and entrapped. Redemption is achieved through knowledge, enlightenment, and the sacraments.

Distinctive Features

The Gospel of Philip is known for its poetic and allegorical style. It often employs metaphorical language, such as light and darkness, bride and bridegroom, and seal and image, to convey its spiritual messages. Additionally, its emphasis on the sacraments, especially the Bridal Chamber, sets it apart from both canonical gospels and many other Gnostic texts.

Relation to Other Gnostic Texts

While the Gospel of Philip shares many themes with other Gnostic writings, such as the nature of the divine, the flawed material world, and the role of knowledge in salvation, its particular focus on sacramental theology and spiritual union makes it unique. It complements other Gnostic texts by offering a different perspective on familiar themes.

The Gospel of Philip provides a window into the rich tapestry of early Christian thought, offering insights that challenge traditional narratives and invite deeper spiritual exploration. Its blend of Christian doctrine, Gnostic cosmology, and sacramental theology makes it a fascinating and essential text for anyone interested in the diversity of early Christian beliefs and practices.

Sacraments and Rituals in the Gospel of Philip

Introduction to Sacramental Theology in Gnosticism
In the context of Gnosticism, sacraments are not merely symbolic rituals but transformative experiences that facilitate the soul's ascent from the material world to the divine realm. The Gospel of Philip, with its unique blend of Gnostic and Christian elements, places a significant emphasis on the sacraments, offering a deeper, esoteric understanding of these practices.

Baptism: The First Step Towards Enlightenment
Symbolism: Baptism in the Gospel of Philip is symbolic of spiritual rebirth and purification. It represents the shedding of the old, material self and the awakening of the inner, spiritual self.
Purpose: Unlike the traditional Christian view of baptism as a rite of initiation and forgiveness of sins, the Gospel of Philip sees it as a transformative experience that awakens the individual's divine spark, allowing them to begin their journey towards gnosis (knowledge).
Practice: The actual ritual might have involved immersion in water, accompanied by prayers and invocations, but its primary focus was on the internal, spiritual transformation of the initiate.

Eucharist: The Mystical Union with the Divine
Symbolism: The Eucharist, or the "bridal feast," as it's sometimes referred to in the Gospel of Philip, symbolizes the believer's union with the divine. The bread and wine are not just the body and blood of Christ but represent the spiritual nourishment and divine essence that feed the soul.
Purpose: The act of partaking in the Eucharist is seen as a means of merging with the divine, experiencing the presence of Christ within, and reinforcing the initiate's commitment to the spiritual path.
Practice: While the ritual might resemble the traditional Christian Eucharist, its interpretation in the Gospel of Philip is more mystical, emphasizing the internal experience over the external ritual.

The Bridal Chamber: The Ultimate Sacrament

Symbolism: The Bridal Chamber is the most distinctive and central sacrament in the Gospel of Philip. It symbolizes the spiritual union between the believer (the bride) and Christ (the bridegroom). This union transcends earthly marriages and represents the soul's ultimate union with the divine.

Purpose: The Bridal Chamber is the culmination of the Gnostic spiritual journey. It represents the final merging of the soul with the divine, transcending the material world and achieving complete spiritual enlightenment.

Practice: The exact nature of the Bridal Chamber ritual remains a subject of debate among scholars. Some believe it was a symbolic ritual, while others suggest it might have involved specific practices or meditations to facilitate the experience of spiritual union.

The sacraments in the Gospel of Philip are not mere rituals but profound spiritual experiences that guide the believer on their journey from the material to the divine. They offer a unique blend of Christian and Gnostic elements, emphasizing personal transformation, spiritual enlightenment, and union with the divine. Through these sacraments, the Gospel of Philip provides a roadmap for the soul's ascent, highlighting the transformative power of gnosis and the importance of inner experience over external ritual.

The Nature of Reality: Gnostic Cosmology in the Gospel of Philip

Introduction to Gnostic Cosmology

Gnostic cosmology offers a unique perspective on the nature of reality, diverging significantly from orthodox Christian views. Central to Gnostic thought is the idea that the material world is not the creation of the supreme God but rather the result of a cosmic fall or error. The Gospel of Philip delves into these concepts, providing insights into the Gnostic understanding of the universe, creation, and the divine.

The Divine Pleroma: The Realm of Fullness

The Pleroma, often referred to as the "Fullness," is the divine realm where the supreme God and various divine emanations or aeons reside. It represents the true, spiritual reality, as opposed to the flawed material world.

The Pleroma is characterized by unity, light, and spiritual perfection. It is devoid of ignorance, suffering, and decay, which are prevalent in the material world.

The Demiurge: The False Creator

In Gnostic cosmology, the Demiurge is a lesser deity, often depicted as ignorant or malevolent, responsible for creating the material world. The Gospel of Philip, like other Gnostic texts, presents the Demiurge as a being who mistakenly believes he is the only god.

The Demiurge's creation is a flawed reflection of the divine Pleroma. He traps divine sparks or souls within material bodies, subjecting them to the limitations and sufferings of the physical realm.

The Material World: A Realm of Illusion

The material world, according to the Gospel of Philip, is a realm of darkness, ignorance, and decay. It is a distorted reflection of the divine Pleroma and serves as a prison for the divine sparks trapped within human souls. The material world's existence is not without purpose. It serves as a testing ground for souls, offering them the opportunity to awaken to their true nature, seek gnosis (knowledge), and return to the divine realm.

The Role of Jesus and Redemption

Jesus, in the Gospel of Philip and other Gnostic texts, is seen as a divine emissary sent from the Pleroma to awaken humanity to its true nature and offer a path to redemption.

Jesus imparts secret teachings and mysteries that provide the knowledge (gnosis) necessary for souls to transcend the material world's limitations and return to the divine realm.

The Gospel of Philip's Gnostic cosmology presents a dualistic view of reality, contrasting the flawed material world with the perfect divine realm. Central to this cosmology is the concept of gnosis, the transformative knowledge that empowers souls to break free from the material world's chains and ascend to the Pleroma. Through its teachings on the nature of reality, the Gospel of Philip offers a profound exploration of existence, purpose, and the path to spiritual enlightenment.

The Mystery of Resurrection in the Gospel of Philip

Introduction to Gnostic Resurrection

In Gnostic thought, resurrection is not merely a physical event but a profound spiritual transformation. While orthodox Christianity emphasizes the bodily resurrection of Jesus and the promise of a future resurrection for believers, the Gospel of Philip and other Gnostic texts offer a more mystical interpretation, focusing on the soul's ascent from the material to the divine realm.

Resurrection as Spiritual Awakening

In the Gospel of Philip, resurrection is understood as an inner, spiritual awakening. It signifies the soul's realization of its divine origin and its liberation from the confines of the material world.

The text speaks of those who attain this awakening as experiencing a "living resurrection." Unlike a future resurrection that occurs after death, this is a present reality, attainable here and now through gnosis (knowledge).

The Role of Jesus in the Mystery of Resurrection

The Exemplar: Jesus, in the Gospel of Philip, is the embodiment of the resurrection mystery. His life, death, and resurrection serve as a model for the spiritual journey of every soul. Through his teachings and mysteries, he provides the keys to attaining spiritual resurrection.

The Bridal Chamber: One of the central sacraments in the Gospel of Philip is the Bridal Chamber, which symbolizes the soul's union with the divine. This sacrament is closely linked to the mystery of resurrection, representing the culmination of the soul's spiritual journey.

Resurrection and Reintegration with the Divine

signifies the soul's return to the Pleroma, the divine realm of fullness. It marks the end of the soul's exile in the material world and its reintegration with the divine source. Gnosis, or spiritual knowledge, is the catalyst for resurrection. By understanding one's true nature and the nature of reality, the soul can transcend the material world's limitations and ascend to the divine realm.

Contrasts with Orthodox Views

Bodily vs. Spiritual Resurrection: While orthodox Christianity emphasizes a future bodily resurrection, the Gospel of Philip focuses on a present spiritual resurrection. This distinction reflects the broader Gnostic view that values the spiritual over the material.

The Nature of Salvation: In orthodox Christianity, salvation is often linked to faith in Jesus' sacrificial death and resurrection. In the Gospel of Philip, salvation is achieved through knowledge and inner transformation, with resurrection being a central aspect of this process.

The mystery of resurrection in the Gospel of Philip offers a profound exploration of life, death, and rebirth. It challenges traditional notions of resurrection, emphasizing inner transformation and spiritual ascent over physical events. Through its teachings on this mystery, the Gospel of Philip provides a roadmap for the soul's journey from the material to the divine, highlighting the transformative power of knowledge and the promise of spiritual rebirth.

Jesus in the Gospel of Philip

Introduction: The Gnostic Christ

In the Gospel of Philip, Jesus is presented not just as a historical figure but as a divine emissary, a bringer of gnosis (knowledge), and a symbol of the soul's potential for spiritual enlightenment. His role and teachings in this text differ in many ways from the canonical gospels, offering a unique Gnostic perspective on the Christ figure.

Jesus: The Divine Emissary

Jesus is seen as the embodiment of the divine Logos, the Word or emanation from the supreme God. He descends into the material world to bring knowledge and redemption to humanity.

In the Gospel of Philip, Jesus serves as a bridge between the material realm and the divine Pleroma. He represents the potential for humanity to transcend the material world and return to the divine source.

Jesus' Teachings: The Path to Gnosis

The Gospel of Philip emphasizes the mystical and esoteric teachings of Jesus. He imparts secret knowledge to his disciples, guiding them on the path to spiritual enlightenment.

Jesus often employs symbols, allegories, and parables in his teachings. These are not meant to be taken literally but are tools to convey deeper spiritual truths.

Jesus and the Sacraments

Jesus is portrayed as the initiator of the sacraments, especially the Bridal Chamber. Through these rituals, he offers believers a direct experience of the divine and a taste of the spiritual resurrection.

In the Gospel of Philip, the Eucharist is not just a remembrance of Jesus' sacrifice but a mystical union with the divine. Jesus is the bread and wine, and partaking in the Eucharist is a means of internalizing the divine essence.

Jesus and Mary Magdalene

The Gospel of Philip presents a close relationship between Jesus and Mary Magdalene. She is often referred to as his companion or consort, indicating a deep spiritual bond.

Mary Magdalene is portrayed as a key disciple, privy to Jesus' secret teachings. Her relationship with Jesus challenges traditional Christian narratives and highlights the importance of the divine feminine in Gnostic thought.

The Crucifixion and Resurrection

While the crucifixion and resurrection are central events in Christian theology, the Gospel of Philip interprets them symbolically. The crucifixion represents the soul's entrapment in the material world, and the resurrection symbolizes its liberation and ascent to the divine realm.

Jesus' resurrection is not just a historical event but a demonstration of the "living resurrection" that all souls can achieve through gnosis.

In the Gospel of Philip, Jesus emerges as a multifaceted figure, embodying the divine, imparting secret knowledge, and guiding souls on their spiritual journey. His teachings, relationships, and role in the sacraments provide a unique Gnostic perspective on the Christ figure, challenging traditional narratives and inviting deeper spiritual exploration.

The Bridal Chamber: Symbolism and Significance in the Gospel of Philip

Introduction: The Sacrament of the Bridal Chamber

The Bridal Chamber is one of the most distinctive and central sacraments in the Gospel of Philip. Unlike the more familiar Christian sacraments like baptism and the Eucharist, the Bridal Chamber is deeply rooted in Gnostic theology and cosmology, symbolizing the soul's ultimate union with the divine.

Symbolism of the Bridal Chamber

Spiritual Union: At its core, the Bridal Chamber represents the spiritual union between the believer (the bride) and Christ (the bridegroom). This union transcends earthly marriages and points to a deeper, mystical connection with the divine.

Reintegration with the Pleroma: The sacrament symbolizes the soul's return to the Pleroma, the divine realm of fullness. It marks the end of the soul's journey through the material world and its reintegration with its divine source.

The Hieros Gamos: Drawing from ancient religious traditions, the Bridal Chamber can be seen as a representation of the "Hieros Gamos" or sacred marriage. This is the union of opposites, the merging of the divine masculine and feminine, leading to spiritual wholeness.

The Practice of the Bridal Chamber

A Mystical Ritual: The exact nature of the Bridal Chamber ritual remains a subject of debate among scholars. Some believe it was a symbolic ritual, while others suggest it might have involved specific practices or meditations to facilitate the experience of spiritual union.

Initiation and Enlightenment: The Bridal Chamber was likely reserved for advanced initiates, those who had undergone prior sacraments like baptism and had attained a certain level of gnosis (knowledge). It marked a culmination of the initiate's spiritual journey.

Significance in Gnostic Theology

Overcoming Duality: The Bridal Chamber sacrament embodies the Gnostic goal of transcending the dualities of the material world. Through this union, the soul overcomes the divisions of male and female, light and darkness, spirit, and matter.

The Living Resurrection: In the Gospel of Philip, the experience of the Bridal Chamber is closely linked to the concept of the "living resurrection." It is through this sacrament that believers experience a foretaste of the resurrection, not in the future, but in the present.

The Bridal Chamber and Jesus

Jesus as the Bridegroom: In the Gospel of Philip, Jesus is often referred to as the bridegroom, inviting souls to enter the Bridal Chamber and experience union with the divine.

Mary Magdalene: The close relationship between Jesus and Mary Magdalene in the text can be seen as a symbolic representation of the Bridal Chamber's mysteries. Their spiritual bond exemplifies the deep union that the sacrament aims to achieve.

The Bridal Chamber, with its rich symbolism and profound significance, offers a glimpse into the heart of Gnostic spirituality as presented in the Gospel of Philip. It challenges traditional Christian narratives, emphasizing personal transformation, spiritual enlightenment, and the potential for direct union with the divine. Through its teachings on the Bridal Chamber, the Gospel of Philip provides a roadmap for the soul's journey, highlighting the transformative power of gnosis and the promise of spiritual union.

The Role of Light and Darkness in the Gospel of Philip

Introduction: Dualism in Gnostic Thought

Central to Gnostic cosmology is the concept of dualism, which posits a fundamental distinction between the spiritual and material realms. In the Gospel of Philip, this dualism is often symbolized by the contrasting motifs of light and darkness, representing the divine and the profane, knowledge and ignorance, salvation, and entrapment.

Light: The Symbol of Divine Knowledge

Divine Origin: Light in the Gospel of Philip is often associated with the divine realm, the Pleroma. It represents the pure, unadulterated essence of the supreme God and the aeons.

Gnosis and Enlightenment: Light is symbolic of gnosis, the special knowledge that Gnostics sought. To be "in the light" means to possess this knowledge, to be awakened to one's true divine nature.

Guidance and Illumination: Just as physical light dispels darkness and makes things visible, spiritual light in the Gospel of Philip illuminates the path to salvation, guiding believers out of the darkness of the material world.

Darkness: The Realm of Ignorance and Entrapment

Material World: Darkness symbolizes the material world, which Gnostics viewed as a flawed and imperfect reflection of the divine. It represents the realm of the Demiurge, the false creator, and his archons.

Ignorance: In the Gospel of Philip, darkness is also synonymous with ignorance. Those who are "in the dark" are unaware of their true nature and remain trapped in the cycle of birth, death, and rebirth.

Challenges and Temptations: Darkness embodies the challenges, temptations, and entrapments of the material world that believers must overcome to achieve spiritual enlightenment.

The Interplay of Light and Darkness

The Soul's Journey: The interplay between light and darkness mirrors the soul's journey in Gnostic thought. Souls emanate from the realm of light but become entrapped in the realm of darkness. Through gnosis, they can return to the light.

Jesus as the Bringer of Light: In the Gospel of Philip, Jesus is often portrayed as the bringer of light, the one who comes to dispel the darkness of ignorance and guide souls back to the divine realm.

The Role of Sacraments: Sacraments, such as baptism and the Bridal Chamber, are seen as rituals that help believers move from darkness to light, from ignorance to knowledge.

The motifs of light and darkness in the Gospel of Philip offer profound insights into Gnostic beliefs about the nature of reality, the challenges of the material world, and the path to salvation. These symbols serve as powerful metaphors for the soul's journey, the challenges it faces, and the ultimate goal of reuniting with the divine light. Through its teachings on light and darkness, the Gospel of Philip provides a roadmap for spiritual transformation, emphasizing the importance of knowledge, awareness, and the transcendence of the material realm.

The Gnostic Church vs. Orthodox Christianity in the Gospel of Philip

Introduction: The Landscape of Early Christian Thought

In the early centuries of Christianity, various groups and sects emerged, each with its own interpretation of Jesus' teachings. The Gospel of Philip, a Gnostic text, offers insights into the differences and tensions between the Gnostic Church and what would become Orthodox Christianity.

Foundational Beliefs: Gnosticism vs. Orthodoxy

The two had a different view about the nature of God.

Gnosticism: The Gnostic view posits a supreme, unknowable God and a series of divine emanations or aeons. The material world is the creation of a lesser deity, the Demiurge.

Orthodoxy: Orthodox Christianity believes in a single, omnipotent God who is both transcendent and immanent, creator of both the spiritual and material worlds.

There also were a different view about the role of Jesus.

Gnosticism: Jesus is seen as a divine emissary, a bringer of gnosis (knowledge). His role is to awaken humanity to its true divine nature.

Orthodoxy: Jesus is the Son of God, the second person of the Holy Trinity. His death and resurrection offer salvation to believers.

Finally, there were difference about the nature of Salvation.

Gnosticism: Salvation is achieved through knowledge (gnosis) and inner transformation.

Orthodoxy: Salvation is granted through faith in Jesus' sacrifice and the grace of God.

The Church and Its Sacraments
Gnostic Church:
Sacraments: Gnostic sacraments, like the Bridal Chamber, are deeply symbolic and focus on spiritual transformation and enlightenment.
Authority: Gnostic teachings often rely on direct revelation and personal experience rather than institutional authority.

Orthodox Church:
Sacraments: Orthodox sacraments, like baptism and the Eucharist, are seen as outward signs of inward grace, essential for salvation.
Authority: The Orthodox Church emphasizes apostolic succession and the authority of the bishops and clergy.

Scriptural Interpretations
Gnostic Texts: Gnostic scriptures, like the Gospel of Philip, offer esoteric interpretations of Jesus' teachings, emphasizing inner knowledge and spiritual awakening.
Canonical Texts: The Orthodox Church recognizes the canonical gospels and other New Testament writings, interpreting them in line with established doctrines and traditions.

Tensions and Conflicts
Heresy Accusations: The Orthodox Church often labeled Gnostic beliefs as heretical, leading to tensions and sometimes persecution.
Secret Teachings: Gnostic groups were often secretive, with teachings reserved for initiates, which further deepened the divide with the more public and communal practices of Orthodox Christianity.

The Gospel of Philip, with its Gnostic perspective, highlights the profound differences between the Gnostic Church and Orthodox Christianity. These differences encompass theology, practices, and interpretations of Jesus' teachings. While both traditions sought to understand and follow Jesus' message, their distinct approaches reflect the diverse landscape of early Christian thought. Through its teachings and contrasts, the Gospel of Philip offers a window into the rich tapestry of beliefs and practices that shaped the early Christian world.

The Language and Imagery of the Gospel of Philip

Introduction: The Rich Tapestry of Gnostic Literature

The Gospel of Philip, like many Gnostic texts, is replete with symbolic language, allegories, and vivid imagery. These linguistic and visual tools serve not just as literary devices but as conduits for conveying profound spiritual truths, often esoteric in nature and meant for initiates into Gnostic mysteries.

Symbolic Language: Conveying the Ineffable

The Power of Symbols: In the Gospel of Philip, symbols are not mere representations; they are gateways to deeper understanding. They capture complex spiritual concepts in a form that initiates can meditate upon and derive insights from.

Examples: Common symbols in the text include light (representing knowledge and the divine), darkness (ignorance and the material world), and the bridal chamber (spiritual union and enlightenment).

Allegories: Narratives with Hidden Meanings

Teaching Through Stories: The Gospel often employs allegorical narratives to convey spiritual teachings. These stories, on the surface, might seem simple, but they contain layered meanings meant to guide seekers on their spiritual journey.

The Role of Jesus: In many of these allegories, Jesus plays a central role, often using parables to impart wisdom to his disciples. His teachings, while sometimes cryptic, are meant to provoke introspection and revelation.

Vivid Imagery: Painting the Spiritual Landscape

Descriptive Power: The Gospel of Philip is rich in imagery that paints a vivid picture of Gnostic cosmology, beliefs, and practices. This imagery serves to make abstract concepts tangible and relatable.

Descriptions of the Pleroma as a realm of light and fullness, the material world as a shadowy reflection, and the soul's journey through various realms are all rendered in detailed and evocative imagery.

The Role of Language in Gnostic Rituals

Sacramental Language: The Gospel describes various Gnostic sacraments, and the language used in these rituals is highly symbolic. Words, chants, and prayers are believed to possess transformative power, guiding participants in their spiritual ascent.

Mystical Experiences: The language of the Gospel, especially in the context of rituals, is meant to facilitate mystical experiences. It serves as a bridge between the mundane and the divine, helping initiates transcend the limitations of the material world.

The language and imagery of the Gospel of Philip are not mere literary embellishments. They are integral to the text's purpose, serving as tools for spiritual instruction, meditation, and transformation. Through its rich symbolic language, allegories, and vivid imagery, the Gospel provides a roadmap for seekers, guiding them through the complexities of Gnostic thought and towards the ultimate goal of spiritual enlightenment.

The Historical Context of the Gospel of Philip

Introduction: A Glimpse into Early Christian Diversity
The Gospel of Philip, a prominent Gnostic text, provides invaluable insights into the diverse landscape of early Christianity. To fully appreciate its teachings and significance, it's essential to understand the historical context in which it was written and the broader religious and cultural milieu of the time.

The Rise of Christianity in the Roman Empire

A New Religious Movement: Emerging in the 1st century CE, Christianity began as a small Jewish sect but rapidly expanded, attracting followers from various backgrounds across the Roman Empire.
Persecutions and Challenges: Early Christians often faced persecutions from Roman authorities and skepticism from traditional Jewish communities, leading to a need for defining and defending their beliefs.

The Gnostic Movement

Origins and Beliefs: Gnosticism, a diverse religious movement with roots in Hellenistic Judaism, Platonism, and Eastern religions, emphasized personal spiritual knowledge (gnosis) over orthodox beliefs and rituals.
The Gospel of Philip's Place: As a Gnostic text, the Gospel of Philip reflects this emphasis on inner knowledge, spiritual transformation, and a distinct interpretation of Christian narratives.

Controversies and Canonical Battles

Diverse Christian Writings: The first few centuries of Christianity saw a proliferation of religious texts, each offering different perspectives on Jesus' teachings, his nature, and the path to salvation.
The Formation of the Canon: By the 4th century, the Church began to formalize the New Testament canon, leading to the exclusion of many texts, including Gnostic writings like the Gospel of Philip.

The Discovery of the Nag Hammadi Library

A Historical Revelation: The 1945 discovery of the Nag Hammadi library in Egypt, which included the Gospel of Philip and other Gnostic texts, shed light on the rich tapestry of early Christian thought and the debates that shaped the religion's development.

Re-evaluating Gnosticism: With the availability of primary Gnostic sources, scholars gained a deeper understanding of Gnostic beliefs, practices, and their relationship with orthodox Christianity.

The Broader Cultural and Philosophical Context

Hellenistic Influence: The Gospel of Philip, like many Gnostic texts, reflects the influence of Hellenistic philosophy, especially Platonism, with its emphasis on the dichotomy between the material and spiritual realms.

Interactions with Eastern Religions: Elements of Eastern religions, such as concepts of reincarnation and the cyclical nature of existence, can also be discerned in the Gospel's teachings.

The Gospel of Philip, set against the backdrop of a dynamic and diverse early Christian world, offers a unique perspective on the spiritual and theological debates of its time. Understanding its historical context allows readers to appreciate its depth, significance, and the challenges faced by early Christian communities. The Gospel stands as a testament to the rich tapestry of beliefs that shaped Christianity and offers a window into the spiritual quests of ancient seekers.

The Legacy of the Gospel of Philip

Introduction: A Testament to Gnostic Thought

The Gospel of Philip, one of the most intriguing texts from the Nag Hammadi library, has left an indelible mark on the landscape of Christian Gnosticism and broader spiritual traditions. Its legacy is multifaceted, influencing theological discourse, art, culture, and modern spiritual movements.

Historical Impact: Shedding Light on Early Christianity

Revealing Diverse Beliefs: The Gospel of Philip provides a window into the diverse beliefs and practices of early Christian communities, showcasing the richness of thought during this formative period. Challenging Orthodox Views: By presenting alternative interpretations of Christian narratives and doctrines, the Gospel has played a role in challenging and expanding the orthodox understanding of early Christian beliefs.

Influence on Modern Gnostic Movements

Revival of Ancient Wisdom: The Gospel of Philip, with its profound teachings on gnosis, spiritual transformation, and divine love, has been foundational for the modern revival of Gnosticism.
Guiding New Generations: Contemporary Gnostic groups often turn to the Gospel of Philip for guidance, drawing inspiration from its teachings to shape their practices and beliefs.

Cultural and Artistic Resonance

Inspiring Creativity: The rich symbolism, allegories, and teachings of the Gospel have inspired artists, writers, and musicians, leading to a plethora of works that explore Gnostic themes.
A Touchstone for Exploration: Beyond its religious significance, the Gospel of Philip has become a cultural touchstone, prompting explorations into the nature of reality, love, and spiritual enlightenment.

Theological and Academic Significance

A Subject of Study: The Gospel of Philip has been the focus of extensive academic research, with scholars delving into its origins, historical context, and theological implications.

Broadening Christian Theology: The Gospel's unique perspectives on Jesus, Mary Magdalene, and Christian sacraments have contributed to a broader understanding of Christian theology, encompassing both orthodox and Gnostic views.

Spiritual Legacy: A Path to Inner Knowledge

Guiding Spiritual Journeys: For many spiritual seekers, the Gospel of Philip serves as a guide, offering insights into the nature of the divine, the soul's journey, and the transformative power of knowledge.

Resonating Across Traditions: The universal themes of the Gospel, such as the quest for enlightenment, the nature of love, and the interplay of light and darkness, resonate with various spiritual traditions, making it relevant beyond the confines of Gnosticism.

The legacy of the Gospel of Philip is vast and enduring. From its historical significance as a testament to early Christian diversity to its continued influence on modern spiritual movements, the Gospel stands as a beacon of Gnostic wisdom. Its teachings, which transcend time and cultural boundaries, continue to inspire, challenge, and guide those on a quest for spiritual truth. As humanity navigates the complexities of the modern world, the Gospel of Philip remains a source of timeless wisdom, reminding us of the deeper truths that lie within and the potential for transformation that exists in every soul.

Controversies and Debates in the Gospel of Philip

Introduction: The Turbulent Landscape of Early Christianity
The early Christian era was marked by a plethora of beliefs, doctrines, and interpretations of Jesus' teachings. The Gospel of Philip, as a Gnostic text, was at the heart of many of these debates, challenging orthodox views and offering alternative perspectives on Christian theology and practice.

The Nature of Jesus
Gnostic View: The Gospel of Philip presents Jesus as a divine emissary, a bringer of gnosis (knowledge), and a guide to spiritual enlightenment. His human nature is often downplayed in favor of his divine essence.
Orthodox View: Orthodox Christianity emphasizes both the divinity and humanity of Jesus, viewing him as the incarnate Son of God who died for humanity's sins.

The Role of Mary Magdalene
Gnostic Perspective: The Gospel of Philip portrays Mary Magdalene as a close companion of Jesus, suggesting a deep spiritual bond. She is often seen as a key disciple, privy to Jesus' secret teachings.
Orthodox Perspective: While Mary Magdalene is respected in orthodox circles, her role is less emphasized, and the nature of her relationship with Jesus is not given the same prominence.

Sacraments and Rituals
Gnostic Practices: The Gospel of Philip describes various Gnostic sacraments, such as the Bridal Chamber, which symbolizes the soul's union with the divine. These rituals are deeply symbolic and focus on inner transformation.

Orthodox Practices: Orthodox Christianity has its sacraments, like baptism and the Eucharist, which are seen as essential for salvation. These rituals have a communal aspect and are rooted in the life, death, and resurrection of Jesus.

Scriptural Authority

Gnostic Scriptures: The Gospel of Philip, along with other Gnostic texts, was not included in the canonical New Testament. Gnostics often relied on direct revelation and personal experience as sources of authority.

Orthodox Canon: The Orthodox Church recognizes the canonical gospels and other New Testament writings, emphasizing apostolic tradition and the authority of Church councils in determining the canon.

The Nature of Salvation

Gnostic Salvation: In the Gospel of Philip, salvation is achieved through knowledge (gnosis) and inner transformation. It's a personal journey of enlightenment and realization of one's divine nature.

Orthodox Salvation: In orthodox belief, salvation is granted through faith in Jesus' sacrifice, the grace of God, and participation in the sacraments.

The Gospel of Philip, with its unique perspectives and teachings, was a source of both inspiration and controversy in the early Christian world. Its views on Jesus, Mary Magdalene, sacraments, and salvation often diverged from orthodox beliefs, leading to debates and tensions. These controversies reflect the rich diversity of early Christian thought and the struggles to define the core tenets of the faith. Through its teachings and the debates it sparked, the Gospel of Philip offers a window into the dynamic and evolving landscape of early Christianity.

The Gospel of Philip in Art and Culture

Introduction: The Lasting Impact of Gnostic Texts

The Gospel of Philip, as one of the Gnostic texts, has not only influenced theological debates but has also left its mark on various forms of art and cultural expressions. Its rich symbolism, esoteric teachings, and alternative perspectives on Christian narratives have inspired artists, writers, and thinkers for centuries.

Visual Arts: Painting and Sculpture

Symbolic Representations: The vivid imagery and symbols from the Gospel, such as the Bridal Chamber, light and darkness, and the spiritual union, have been depicted in various artworks, capturing the essence of Gnostic beliefs.

Portrayal of Figures: The Gospel's unique portrayal of figures like Mary Magdalene and Jesus has inspired artists to depict them in a different light, emphasizing their spiritual bond and the deeper mysteries of their teachings.

Literature: Fiction and Poetry

Retelling the Gnostic Narrative: Novelists and poets have been drawn to the Gospel of Philip for its alternative take on biblical events, leading to reinterpretations and imaginative retellings of these stories.

Exploring Spiritual Themes: The Gospel's emphasis on inner knowledge, spiritual awakening, and the soul's journey has resonated with writers, leading to works that delve into these themes and the quest for enlightenment.

Music: Compositions and Songs

Sacred Music: The Gospel's teachings, especially its sacraments and rituals, have inspired composers to create sacred music that captures the essence of Gnostic spirituality.

Modern Interpretations: Contemporary musicians, drawn to the Gospel's mystical and esoteric nature, have incorporated its themes and imagery into songs and compositions, blending ancient wisdom with modern sounds.

Film and Theater

Dramatizing the Gnostic Quest: The Gospel of Philip's narrative, with its spiritual quests, challenges, and revelations, lends itself to dramatic interpretations. Playwrights and filmmakers have explored its themes, bringing the Gnostic journey to life on stage and screen.

Exploring Relationships: The Gospel's portrayal of relationships, especially the bond between Jesus and Mary Magdalene, has been a subject of interest, leading to productions that delve into the complexities of love, spirituality, and enlightenment.

Modern Culture and Spirituality

The Gospel of Philip, along with other Gnostic texts, has played a role in the modern revival of Gnosticism. Its teachings resonate with those seeking alternative spiritual paths and a deeper understanding of Christian mysticism.

Elements from the Gospel have been incorporated into New Age teachings, emphasizing personal spiritual experiences, the divine feminine, and the quest for inner knowledge.

The Gospel of Philip, with its rich tapestry of symbols, teachings, and narratives, has left an indelible mark on art and culture. Its influence extends beyond theological debates, touching the realms of creativity and cultural expression. Through various forms of art, the Gospel's timeless wisdom and spiritual insights continue to inspire and resonate with audiences across the ages.

Modern Gnosticism and the Gospel of Philip

Introduction: The Resurgence of Ancient Wisdom
In the contemporary era, there has been a renewed interest in ancient spiritual traditions, including Gnosticism. The Gospel of Philip, with its profound teachings and alternative Christian perspectives, has played a pivotal role in this modern Gnostic revival.

The Discovery of the Nag Hammadi Library
The 1945 discovery of the Nag Hammadi library in Egypt, which included the Gospel of Philip among other Gnostic texts, was a watershed moment. It provided scholars and spiritual seekers with direct access to primary Gnostic sources that had been lost for centuries.

With the availability of these texts, there was a renewed academic and popular interest in Gnosticism, leading to a re-evaluation of its teachings, practices, and historical significance.

Modern Gnostic Movements
Modern Gnostic movements often position themselves as alternative Christianities, emphasizing personal spiritual experiences, direct knowledge of the divine, and a reinterpretation of biblical narratives. As one of the key texts from the Nag Hammadi library, the Gospel of Philip has become foundational for many modern Gnostic groups. Its teachings on the nature of reality, the role of Jesus, and the significance of sacraments like the Bridal Chamber resonate with contemporary seekers.

The Gospel of Philip in Contemporary Spirituality
The Gospel's emphasis on inner knowledge and personal transformation aligns with modern spiritual trends that prioritize individual experiences over institutional dogma.
The Gospel of Philip, with its syncretic blend of Christian, Platonic, and Eastern philosophies, has found a place in interfaith dialogues, bridging gaps between different spiritual traditions.

Modern Interpretations and Adaptations

The Gospel of Philip has inspired modern writers to explore Gnostic themes in fiction, poetry, and essays, bringing its ancient wisdom to new audiences.

From visual arts to film and music, the Gospel's teachings and imagery have been adapted and reimagined, reflecting its enduring appeal and relevance.

Challenges and Criticisms

Orthodox Pushback: As with ancient Gnosticism, modern Gnostic movements, and their reliance on texts like the Gospel of Philip, often face criticism from orthodox Christian groups who view them as heretical or inauthentic.

Historical Authenticity: Some scholars caution against reading the Gospel of Philip as a historical document, emphasizing its symbolic and allegorical nature.

The Gospel of Philip, once lost to history, has found a new life in the modern era. Its teachings, which challenge traditional Christian narratives and offer a path of personal spiritual discovery, resonate with contemporary seekers. As modern Gnosticism continues to grow and evolve, the Gospel of Philip remains a testament to the enduring power of ancient wisdom and the human quest for the divine.

Conclusion: The Timeless Wisdom of the Gospel of Philip

A Gnostic Gem

The Gospel of Philip, with its profound teachings, allegories, and insights, stands as a testament to the depth and richness of Gnostic thought. Its wisdom, though rooted in ancient traditions, continues to resonate with seekers across ages, cultures, and spiritual paths.

The Universal Quest for Knowledge

Gnosis as a Path: At the heart of the Gospel of Philip is the concept of gnosis, or knowledge. This is not just intellectual knowledge but a deep, transformative understanding of one's true nature and the nature of reality.

Relevance Today: In an age of information overload, the Gospel's emphasis on inner knowledge and personal revelation offers a refreshing perspective, reminding readers of the importance of introspection and spiritual awakening.

The Gospel's Vision of Love and Unity

Divine Relationships: The Gospel of Philip delves into the nature of divine relationships, especially the bond between Jesus and Mary Magdalene. It offers a vision of love that transcends the physical, pointing to a spiritual union.

Modern Implications: In a world often divided by differences, the Gospel's teachings on love, unity, and spiritual connection offer a blueprint for harmonious coexistence and mutual understanding.

Challenging Orthodox Narratives

Alternative Perspectives: The Gospel of Philip provides alternative interpretations of well-known Christian narratives, challenging orthodox views and encouraging readers to question and explore.

Enduring Appeal: This willingness to challenge established beliefs, to seek truth beyond dogma, gives the Gospel of Philip its enduring appeal, especially for those who value independent thought and spiritual exploration.

The Gospel's Influence on Art and Culture

Timeless Inspiration: As previously discussed, the Gospel of Philip has inspired countless artists, writers, and thinkers, its rich symbolism and profound teachings serving as a wellspring of creativity.

A Cultural Touchstone: Beyond its spiritual teachings, the Gospel has become a cultural touchstone, reflecting humanity's age-old quest for meaning and connection.

The Path Forward

Continued Relevance: As spiritual seekers continue to search for authentic paths of enlightenment, the Gospel of Philip, with its emphasis on personal revelation, inner transformation, and divine love, remains a guiding light.

A Living Tradition: While the Gospel is an ancient text, its teachings are very much alive, continually adapted and reinterpreted by modern Gnostic movements, spiritual teachers, and individual seekers.

Final Thoughts

The Gospel of Philip, with its timeless wisdom, serves as a bridge between the ancient and the modern, the material and the spiritual. It reminds readers of the eternal truths that lie within and the potential for transformation that exists in every soul. As humanity continues its spiritual journey, the Gospel of Philip stands as a beacon, illuminating the path to enlightenment and the realization of our true divine nature.

Printed in Great Britain
by Amazon

35850848R00132